PRESIDING OVER
SHADOWS

FROM CHAOS
TO ORDER IN THE COURT

MICHAEL RANDAZZO

WILDBLUE
PRESS

WildBluePress.com

PRESIDING OVER SHADOWS published by:
WILDBLUE PRESS
P.O. Box 102440
Denver, Colorado 80250

WILDBLUE PRESS is registered at the U.S. Patent and Trademark Offices.

ISBN 978-1-964730-72-1 Hardcover
ISBN 978-1-964730-73-8 Trade Paperback
ISBN 978-1-964730-71-4 eBook
Cover design © 2025 WildBlue Press. All rights reserved.

Interior Formatting and Book Cover Design by Elijah Toten
www.totencreative.com

PRESIDING OVER
SHADOWS

CONTENTS

FOREWORD

Chaos was in their blood, or so it seemed. My family has been a lot of different things. To most, *what* they were mattered more than *who* they were. They were miscreants, deviants, mafiosos, dealers, goons, racketeers, and molesters, but many forget they were also caregivers, mothers, fathers, uncles, aunts, grandparents, lovers, friends, and protectors. Can one love a person unconditionally, without condoning their actions? What if that person is in your family?

I am cut from that same cloth—but you couldn't tell that from the smooth-pressed wool of the black robe that I wear each day. Despite my family baggage, I am honored to serve as the Division 2 Circuit Judge for of the 42nd Judicial Circuit in the state of Missouri. The office that robe signifies is the very mechanism I have used to prevent my past from finding its way into my present.

Most days, my life is amazing. I live on a farm with my wife Amanda, stepson Jacob, son Joey (Michael Jr.), and daughter Gracie. We share this property with my brother Kevin, his wife Treasure, my niece Klarissa, and my nephew Karson. Randazzo Ranch, as we've christened it, is nestled between state parks in rural Missouri.

Large windows adorn each of the courthouses where I work. The sun's rays, when angled just right, cast long shadows into the courtroom. In our justice system, for one side to feel the sun, the other must be engulfed in darkness. When I feel the sun's warmth on my face, I know something behind me is being eclipsed. For most of my family's history, chaos kept us on the wrong side of the law, the place where insiders benefit from the lack of light. Those are the shadows over which I preside.

Let me be absolutely clear: I have never been associated with the crimes of my ancestors. Overcoming that genetic predisposition has been a lifelong battle. While a name can open doors for some, mine has been a burden, a shadow cast by the misdeeds of my forefathers. By acknowledging their sins, my aim isn't to shame them, but rather to shield future generations from the deviance that seems woven into our family's DNA. The Randazzos were, for a time, associated with the Mafia—though I never was. That's always been my struggle.

I long to be seen as grateful—not because I want the label, but because I *am*. As a lawyer, I was appointed many times to represent indigent clients, and, even though I could have, I refused to charge any of them for my representation. This was an unwise business decision, but its impact upon those clients was monumental. Other than the appointing judge, no other soul knew I was working on those cases for free. I didn't want recognition; I just wanted to help.

Our brains crave to assign labels to those around us; they help us categorize, generalize, and draw quick conclusions—a survival mechanism from simpler times. But labels can also trap us, reducing our perspective to black-and-white caricatures in a world awash with shades of gray.

Think of the word "judge." What springs to mind? An old white man in a black robe, gavel in hand? Or do you picture a judge you know personally? Our presumptions are shaped by our connections. We are so much more than any single label can convey.

The labels assigned to us are hard to shake. I've spent a lifetime trying to escape the ones attached to my name. Those labels weren't undeserved by my ancestors—but how does one shed a preconception? Changing minds is a herculean task. Confirmation bias kicks in, causing people to focus only on evidence that supports their existing view and ignore anything to the contrary. Despite all this, we have to try: I chose a career in law knowing that success in a legitimate field would be the most effective way to distance myself from my family's past.

The day I began writing this book, I was driving home, noticing the first hints of autumn. Soon, the Ozark Mountains would be ablaze with reds, yellows, and oranges. A tiny fox squirrel clutching an acorn darted across the potholed road. I swerved to avoid hitting it, and the near-miss got me thinking.

Imagine that squirrel's perspective. It carefully planned its crossing, sensing no danger; then, halfway across, its life was almost snuffed out by an inattentive human.

Some drivers wouldn't have seen the squirrel in time to swerve. Others wouldn't have bothered. Statistically, that squirrel was lucky. But did it realize how close it came to oblivion? Was it unfazed by the near-death experience? Did it deserve to be saved? Perhaps it was oblivious to the chaos around it, to its place in the grand scheme of things, to the fact that a plan exists for every being.

Perhaps God's greatest gift is that of self-awareness: the understanding of how undeserving we are of existence. Knowing that we exist against all odds keeps us from dwelling on what we lack, and helps us appreciate what we have. With this perspective, I find meaning and connections where others might not. My story is about these connections, the ones that have shaped my extraordinary life. These connections, of course, come with labels.

Just as darkness is the opposite of light, chaos the opposite of order. My journey from anarchy began in 1984, but the chaos predates my birth. Darkness and chaos have always existed, and they will persist long after I'm gone. This is a story of choices, traumas, lessons, and sacrifices, all made in the pursuit of a better life. The stories within are intertwined, each one rippling outward and influencing the next. I am both a beneficiary and a prisoner of my family's legacy; I've dedicated my life to outrunning it, and leaving one that my children won't have to flee.

OUR THING

Sicilian culture ingrained in us the importance of *famiglia*. As life has taught me, family isn't always about blood; it's about support, love, trust, and a mutual sense of duty. Families protect their own, and that requires keeping secrets. A prerequisite for joining the Mafia was swearing omertà, a death pledge of silence and loyalty to the family above all else. It meant rejecting any cooperation with law enforcement—loose lips sink ships, after all. It sealed a lifetime commitment from which death was the only escape. In a way, this book is a betrayal of that oath my ancestors took. But I hope that bringing some of these secrets to light will be liberating; not just for me, but for those whose stories are intertwined with mine. My intent isn't to embarrass or burden anyone, but to dismantle the labels and set the record straight.

To understand my story, a history lesson is in order. "Our thing"—La Cosa Nostra, more universally known as the Mafia—began in the 1800s, during the unification of Sicily and mainland Italy. Before this, feudal lords ruled Sicily, each with their own dominion. The people relied on their lords for protection.

The unification allowed citizens to start businesses and own land. But this newfound wealth brought with it a new problem: how would the landowners protect their property?

The lords no longer provided this service, and in the late 1870s, theft ran rampant.

Separated from the mainland by sea, Sicily lacked the same governmental control over illicit activity. The distinction between Italians and Sicilians mattered greatly before the 20th century. My own family felt this divide: my great-grandmother, Rose Benigno, a Sicilian, was ostracized for marrying my great-grandfather, Joseph Randazzo, an Italian. Physical differences also set them apart: Sicilians tended to have darker skin, eyes, and hair, while mainlanders were lighter. Sicilians were proud of their heritage and resisted being lumped together with the mainlanders. They even spoke their own language, a dialect distinct from mainstream Italian.

Out of necessity, groups on the island united to protect each other's property. Those who couldn't protect themselves paid others to do it for them. These protectors became skilled at their task, and eventually, they realized the need for formal organization. The protector clans began to coalesce, electing bosses who resembled the feudal lords of Sicily's past. Power soon concentrated in these figures, and over time the organizations adopted a loose military structure: soldiers at the base, lieutenants above them, and bosses at the apex; "don," derived from the Italian *dominus* ("lord"), became the infamous title for these powerful men. The dons began as saviors, devolved into exploiters, and, just before their downfall, became despots.

When mass migrations from Italy and Sicily surged in the late 1800s and early 1900s, the ideals of these homelands crossed the Atlantic. But immigrants who left seeking a better life encountered instead discrimination and prejudice. Americans, often failing to distinguish between the various groups, lumped them together as "Italians" and blamed them for the country's ills. Italians were often segregated into their own neighborhoods, which began to spring up across the United States.

These new neighborhoods became targets for exploitation by nativist Americans, who knowingly took advantage of the immigrants they deemed undesirable. Again, facing exploitation and thievery, the Italian communities needed protection. With the necessary elements in place, La Cosa Nostra (LCN) brought its organization to American shores. It was poised to become the most formidable international crime syndicate the world had ever seen. Among those arriving during this period of expansion were my great-grandparents, Rose Benigno and Joseph (Guiseppe) Randazzo, the parents of my Grandpa Nick.

Giuseppe was born on a ship en route to America; his mother, Dominica Laffata, had fled Sicily for a fresh start, leaving his father behind. According to maritime law, citizenship was determined by the port of departure, so Giuseppe was considered an Italian.

Upon arrival at Ellis Island, Dominica, who spoke little English, tried her best to communicate with immigration officials. She carried paperwork documenting her name and parentage, but Giuseppe, having been born at sea, had no such documents. Dominica slowly pronounced "Giu-Sepp," but the officials, their American ears unaccustomed to Italian inflection, recorded his first name as "Joseph." Dominica further explained that they were from the town of Randazzo in Sicily, exclaiming "Randazzo! Randazzo!" The officials, mistaking it for a last name, wrote it down as well.

This mix-up resulted in my great-grandfather being forever known as Joseph "Joe" Randazzo. It's a fitting irony that the way his name was assigned to him mirrored the unjust placement of labels upon his descendants, forever tying them to an inescapable past. Dominica and Joe settled in Chicago, and later St. Louis, Missouri. Chicago in the 1920s and 30s was a tough city, home to Alphonse "Al" Gabriel Capone, arguably the most notorious criminal in American history and a figure revered by many Italians. Al Capone directly influenced the future of my family, employing a lieutenant named Michael Benigno—my great-great-uncle Mike, my namesake.

AN UNMADE MAN

Joe would find his place in an Italian neighborhood, where families lived, worked, and protected each other—just as their ancestors had done in the old country. The parallels were striking: new land, same struggles, same solutions. Shortly after arriving in America, Dominica married Dominic Biondo, a "made" man in the St. Louis Mafia. Biondo would become more than just a stepfather to Joe; he would become "Dad," a title Joe would use until his dying day. He would also become the namesake of my grandfather.

When Joe was nineteen years old, he met Rose Benigno, the woman who would become his lifelong companion. She was sixteen when they married, their union a Romeo and Juliet tale that sparked controversy between their families. The distinction between Sicilian and Italian blood, although it seems trivial today, created a rift that threatened to tear them apart. But love, as it often does, prevailed.

Rose came from Kankakee, a Chicago suburb where her family had dropped anchor, but marriage swept her away. Her brother, Michael "Mike" Benigno, who for a time remained in Kankakee, became a significant figure in the Chicago Outfit. His connection to Al Capone gave him street credibility that would prove valuable in the years to come.

The marriage of Rose and Joe did more than unite two hearts—it created a bridge between the Benigno and Biondo families. Uncle Mike's reputation, earned through his service to Capone, made him a natural fit with the Biondos. At Rose's urging, Mike relocated to St. Louis, setting in motion events that would lead to the first Randazzo being "made."

Joe had grown up in the shadow of the Mafia. His stepfather, Dominic Biondo, held the rank of lieutenant in the St. Louis Mafia, the local chapter of the Sicilian-American Mafia. It was a position that Joe's uncles and brother would eventually share, and that Joe himself would come to hold. But the path wasn't free of obstacles—formal admission required sponsorship, and being of Italian heritage wasn't enough. The Biondos, despite having raised Joe as their own, were unwilling to sponsor him: he was not their blood.

It was Mike Benigno who finally opened the door. After Joe's marriage to Rose, the two men grew close, developing a bond more like brothers than in-laws. Mike's sponsorship led to Joe being voted in, and with the swearing of omertà, Joe became a "made" man. This oath bound him to the organization's command structure, placing him under the oversight of Mike and the Biondos.

Joe proved himself a capable soldier, but the specifics of his activities remain shrouded in mystery. Such matters were never discussed outside the organization, so no record exists. The oath of silence wasn't just a promise; it was a way of life, one that would echo through generations.

One thing we do know: my great-grandfather, Joseph Randazzo, was a convicted felon. How he ended up in prison never made sense to me. The story Joe told his family differed greatly from the details of his conviction that

I would later uncover. Grandpa Nick told the story of his dad's guilty plea and subsequent incarceration.

It began when Grandpa Joe received a phone call from his brother-in-law, Mike, with a specific task: pick up a truckload of freshly-picked apples and drive them a long distance to a waiting buyer. Because apples have a short shelf life, they needed to be delivered quickly, which incentivized distributors to skip some licensing and regulatory compliance steps. The truck and its load would have to avoid inspection by the authorities.

Joe agreed to transport the apples for a hefty price. Everything went according to plan until he was almost back to St. Louis. Joe's cargo was covered by a heavy tarp, but some apples fell out of the truck bed and onto the road right as he was passing a police officer. The officer pursued and pulled Joe over. Unable to produce registration for the load, an investigation began into the source of the apples. The source couldn't be verified, so Grandpa Joe was charged with a felony: illegal transportation of cargo across state lines. Unable to defend his actions in court, he was convicted.

For years, the family accepted the apple story as the truth, but I was always skeptical. Prison for apples? Maybe a fine, but prison time seemed so disproportionate that my instincts told me there was more to the story. The incident seemed more like a clandestine operation than a simple regulatory mishap, and I knew of a certain something that could land you in deep trouble if you were caught transporting it across state lines. So, I began to search through the archives, looking for anything associated with the "apple fiasco." After a thorough investigation, I found my answer.

"Joseph Randazzo, a man associated with the St. Louis Mafia, was convicted of distribution of heroin," the newspaper clipping read. The rest was illegible, but my suspicions had been proven correct. "Apples" were heroin. My great-grandfather was a heroin mule for the St. Louis Mafia.

As a reward for keeping his mouth shut, the men Joe worked for took good care of Grandma Rose and the Randazzo kids, providing them with money and housing while Joe was in prison. Upon his release, Grandpa Joe was back at it. To assist in his unlawful pursuits, Grandpa Joe became the sole proprietor of a taxicab company. Grandpa Nick insisted that the company was called "Yellow Cab"—I only repeat the name because Grandpa Nick was so adamant about it. The company was gifted to Grandpa Joe after he served time in prison in lieu of his bosses. It was a good front: the constant stream of riders and locations provided cover for frequenting certain places and dropping off passengers and packages. The business was an efficient way to wash dirty money. And it offered a ready excuse for why a package full of illicit substances might be found in the backseat: a random rider must have left it there. At a time when passenger records were never kept, this explanation was often accepted at face value.

Yellow Cab was profitable, and Grandpa Joe's fleet grew to hundreds of vehicles at its peak. However, the success was short-lived. Grandpa Joe was a gambler, addicted to wagering on chance. My father recalls going to the horse races with Grandpa Joe almost every day, where he would bet on each race. He never knew when to quit, and he almost always returned home empty-handed. His gambling addiction ultimately led to the demise of his company. Joe often met up with his rich friends and engaged in high-stakes gambling: sometimes dice, but most often cards. Joe began to bet ownership of his cabs. One by one, he gambled away every asset of his company.

Yellow Cab was a great front, but it also represented Joe's only hope to go legit: if he had grown the business, he could have made a living from it—a legal, clean income. As these hopes vanished, Joe took stock of his situation. He and Rose had, at this point, eight children: Frank, Joseph Jr., Sam, Nick, Mayme, Patricia, Francis, and Florence (Rosemary, a ninth, had died in childhood due to a congenital defect). Frank and Joseph Jr., his oldest sons, had already been granted membership in the "family" business; Sam and Nick would be following them soon. Joe had spent time in jail. His brother-in-law and mentor, Mike, had also been imprisoned. And now, his gambling had taken away his only source of above-board income. He was in too deep, but he knew that death was the only way out of the Mafia. With all this in mind, Grandpa Joe made an unthinkable request of the mob bosses.

Joe worked with Mike Benigno to get the Randazzos out of the organization. He pleaded his case up the line, all the way to the don, and eventually, an exception was made to allow the Randazzos to leave. In exchange for this separation, the Randazzos would be dead to the Mafia; they were not to speak of the organization, even to family members.

While Grandpa Joe took this covenant very seriously, Grandpa Nick just couldn't keep his mouth shut. He shared countless childhood stories full of vivid details about the family business. He remembered riding with his dad to collect stacks of money from businesses, then dropping the money off elsewhere. He also recounted being rushed out of a restaurant by his father during what he described as a "hit."

Even more vividly, he described how the "family" would unwind: large card games every weekend, with dapperly-dressed, middle-aged mob bosses seated around the table. Each had their stack of cash, a beverage, and a pistol.

The pistols served two purposes: deterring cheating and providing ready access to a weapon in case of a rival's assassination attempt.

During one of these games, Grandpa Nick overheard something significant, something he never forgot: a discussion about "the plates." He recalled Uncle Mike asking Grandpa Joe, "You've got those plates hid here, right?" Joe replied, "Ya. They're hidden in the walls. Coppers will never find them." Grandpa Nick pondered the significance of the plates and wondered why they were hidden. Why would the police be interested? Based on the conversation, he knew they had value, and he became determined to find them.

He waited for the house to empty before beginning his search, meticulously examining every nook and cranny. What exactly did his dad mean by "in the walls?" His investigation led him to scrutinize the structure of the house itself. In a room adorned with wallpaper, he noticed a section that appeared to be lifting away from the wall. He approached and inspected the anomaly. Jackpot! He peeled back the wallpaper to reveal a small, hidden door. Opening it, he discovered his treasure: stacks of odd-looking molds, each stamped in the form of different denominations of currency. $1s, $10s, $20s, $50s, $100s—they were all there. Remembering the money his dad had picked up and dropped off, he connected the dots: they were literally printing money. It wouldn't be long before the government reached the same conclusion.

The FBI and Secret Service were constantly documenting Mike Benigno's whereabouts and activities. Aware of their presence, Mike would always announce whether he was being tailed. If he was, there would be no discussion of business, only coded conversations. But even the code would eventually be broken.

Jealousy, rivalry, and self-preservation lead to the downfall of even the most powerful syndicates. Infiltrating the Italian Mafia had proved challenging for government agents, but their patience eventually paid off: as is the case in every large criminal investigation, eventually, someone snitched. The Secret Service learned that large quantities of counterfeit bills were circulating in the St. Louis area, and were often passed in Italian neighborhoods, particularly near the Hill.

The Hill was the heart of the Italian community in St. Louis, where most Italians lived, worked, and worshipped. The Secret Service began to monitor businesses on the Hill, sending in undercover agents to catch those spreading the fake bills. During this surveillance, an associate of the St. Louis Mafia was arrested for assault. While booking him, they discovered counterfeit bills in his possession. Knowing his movements that day, federal agents armed with search warrants raided the businesses and homes of syndicate members.

In a warehouse, they found the evidence they needed: the inks, paper, and printing presses. The ink was tested and confirmed to match the ink used on the counterfeit bills already in the government's possession. The only missing piece was the plates, tucked away in the walls of the Randazzo home.

The warehouse where the operation was discovered was leased to Mike Benigno. Uncle Mike was apprehended and questioned, but, true to his oath, he remained silent during the interrogation. His refusal to talk guaranteed that Uncle Mike wouldn't leave a free man. He was arrested and charged with counterfeiting.

The Mafia's operation was massive, printing hundreds of thousands of dollars per day. Counterfeiting served a crucial purpose for the organization, generating vast sums of money that could be passed off as legitimate. Printing your own money was far easier than earning it. But now, their operation was shut down, and its members were at risk of indictment.

Uncle Mike consulted with the group. Knowing that it would deflect attention from the others, Mike took one for the team and pleaded guilty to counterfeiting. He was sentenced to sixty months in prison. Upon his term's completion, he was made a don of the Florida syndicate. For his loyalty and discretion, Uncle Mike was set up for life, forever in favor with the mob.

The Randazzos, however, were completely "unmade." I recall Grandpa Nick being upset by this separation. He had no qualms about what he would have chosen if the decision hadn't been made for him: Grandpa Nick would have been a mobster. Fortunately for the generations that followed, he wouldn't get the chance to be "made."

The irony isn't lost on me that, in two generations, my family has turned 180 degrees, from crime and chaos to law and order. I often reflect on the impact the excommunication had on my life. My brother, Kevin, and my wife, Amanda, are police officers. I have been a child abuse investigator, a prosecuting attorney, and a judge. If Grandpa Joe hadn't been excommunicated, we would likely have been unable to pursue those careers—and even if we did, our family members would have shunned us.

BIG NICK

Legally, he was known as Dominick Joseph Randazzo. To most, he was Big Nick. To me, he was everything. I called him Grandpa Nick. The youngest child of Italian immigrants, Joseph and Rose, he looked the part. He had striking blue eyes, the hue of which I sometimes recall when I look up at a bright sky. He was a "greaseball," with slicked-back, jet-black hair reminiscent of his hero, Elvis Presley. He commanded attention in any room. Broad-shouldered, with hands like gorilla paws, he was a unit of a man. He had to be: it took a lot to carry the burdens of this family on his back. Grandpa Nick was the lynchpin of our family, demanding respect when he spoke, the final arbiter of all disputes. He was my hero.

He knew how to weave a story: start with background, build anticipation, add humor, and resolve the conflict with a comedic and humble touch. I want to share one of those stories.

My grandfather thought he was invincible. I always thought the same, until the day I delivered his eulogy. It was hard to see him as anything less than a stabilizing force, an opinionated yet caring and giving grandfather. Having heard the tales of his rebellious antics, I know he was a troublemaker, often challenged by the recipients of his ill-conceived pranks, a jokester who seldom knew when he'd crossed the line. This trait must be genetic, as similar dispositions often appear among the males of my family.

His overconfidence as a pugilist led him to challenge many men he shouldn't have, but he never met his match. Hoping to find an equal, he turned to the animal kingdom. One day, Grandpa Nick saw an advertisement for a sideshow exhibition, the main event of which was grizzly bear wrestling. No normal human would even consider fighting a grizzly, but Big Nick Randazzo was no normal human. The prize for defeating this monster was significant: glory, $10,000, and an all-expenses-paid trip to Las Vegas.

In the days leading up to the event, Grandpa Nick was ridiculed by his brother Sam, Grandma Janelle, and anyone else who heard his plan. Convinced that he was strong enough to hurt the bear but that his cardio needed work, he jogged around the block puffing a Winchester Little Cigar. Fueled by encouragement and nicotine, he marched toward the fight.

The bout was quite a spectacle. Grandpa Nick and Uncle Sam drove miles out of town, down a gravel road, into a farmer's field. Circles of cars surrounded the ring, scores of people eager to see a grizzly bear in person. The match and the lucrative reward had drawn a capacity crowd. Spectators paid $1 for entry, and competitors paid $20 for a shot at the champion.

Upon arrival, Grandpa Nick registered for his debut in the ring later that day and took his place ringside. He'd been to many matches at the St. Louis Arena, and this ring was no less professional than the one in which he'd watched Dick the Bruiser dominate. A ringmaster in a business suit made his way to the center and announced the rules of the bout, listing them off to cheers and jests.

First, the bear would always wear a muzzle. Second, participants could use any method to try to pin the bear. Third, a pin occurred when the bear's back was flat on the ring's surface with the participant on top. Last, no weapons.

The ringmaster called the bear out. A meek-looking teenager walked toward the center of the crowd, leading the behemoth out with a leather leash. The ringmaster announced the official measurements: "Weighing in at 1,000 pounds and with a height of ten feet tall, the undisputed Grizzly Wrestling Champion, The Nightmare of the Yukon, Horrible Harry!" (I once felt compelled to look up how large grizzly bears actually get, knowing Grandpa could exaggerate a story from time to time. Let's just say they don't get quite that big.)

Harry entered the ring on all fours, a large metal contraption strapped over his mouth and nose and around the back of his enormous skull. Beneath the device, butter-yellow fangs were stained dark red with what appeared to be blood. Surely, that muzzle was the only thing protecting his opponents from being ripped to shreds.

On command, Harry stretched out his hind legs and took the stance of a typical human boxer. The glaring sun was eclipsed by the brown fur of the natural killer in his corner. The ringmaster called the name of the first contestant, a scrawny man who trembled with fear as he entered the ring. The match began, and he was quickly dispatched by a left paw to the head. He exited as quickly as he'd entered.

Sam and Nick watched as man after man was defeated by the giant. While Sam began to doubt the wisdom of letting his little brother take a shot at the title, Nick's confidence only grew as he learned from the mistakes of each contestant. He was determined to enter the ring aggressively, wind up his best right hook, knock the bear unconscious, and then walk over and pin his foe. He was already pondering how he'd divide the spoils.

His chance arrived. The announcer called out, "Our next contestant, Nick RON-DAY-ZO!" He shook his head as he approached. The announcer made the same mistake everyone did. "It's Ran-DA-zoh," Grandpa Nick corrected. (Having heard our name mispronounced so many times in my own life, I wonder if it would be easier to just go with the common pronunciation.) Nick entered the ring with the swagger of Muhammad Ali, bouncing around in imitation of "The World's Greatest." The bell rang, and a stare-down ensued as the fighters locked eyes. Grandpa Nick raised his dukes and prepared for battle. As Harry approached, Nick swung his right fist, making solid contact. This was the shot he'd been waiting for. Grandpa backed away to allow the next step of his plan to play out, but the bear dismissed the blow with a flinch and a shake, as if a housefly had landed on his nose.

That wasn't the plan. But Nick wasn't a quitter, and he was determined to land another strike. The trainer barked a command at Harry, who responded with a deep, echoing growl. Grandpa was in trouble. The bear advanced more quickly than Nick could prepare for and took hold of the Italian. Chest to face, Harry squeezed his opponent in a literal bear hug until the command was given to release him. Nick lay on the canvas until he could breathe again. The bear returned to his corner. Having the breath squeezed from their lungs would have made most men give up, but Nick rose with one last surge of energy and ran toward Harry. Just before Nick connected with a knockout punch, Harry swung his paw in a backhand motion. The knuckles and claws struck with such force that Grandpa was launched into the air and back into his own corner. He was done. A towel came flying over the ropes. Sam entered the ring, saving his sibling from further devastation at the hands of the "Nightmare of the Yukon."

More than once, I heard the brothers quarrel over the events of that day. Grandpa Nick was convinced he would have knocked that "son of a bitch" out if he'd been given another chance. Uncle Sam was convinced he'd saved his brother from serious injury and further humiliation. The conversation often ended with the two discussing the trick to beating the trained bear. A human champion *was* crowned that day. A young kid, maybe a teenager, entered the ring with the bear and gently sprawled himself out on the ground. The bear mimicked the action. The two lay next to each other for a moment, and then the human reached over and softly stroked the bear's fur. He then placed his arm and shoulder over the beast's chest. The bear remained motionless. The ringmaster shouted, "1, 2, 3!" The boy had won.

I find great meaning in that story. I take away the lesson that you should never think you're invincible. More importantly, you shouldn't face the world with aggression, because, like the bear, life will beat you down. However, if you approach the world with calculation and gentleness, life will respond in kind.

FIRST FELONY

Grandpa Nick had always been a gearhead. His love of automobiles came from his father: he spent his youth helping Grandpa Joe in the maintenance shop where he took care of the fleet of cabs he once owned. After his excommunication from the St. Louis Mafia, Grandpa Joe installed tires for patrons at that same shop. Nick had a tremendous mind for numbers. Even on his deathbed, he would rattle off phone numbers he'd memorized throughout his life, each accompanied by a name and the significance of its remembrance. He also had a knack for knowing the value of any vehicle. From the age of fourteen, Grandpa Nick had always owned a car. When he didn't own one, he would steal one.

One time, around the age of fifteen, Grandpa Nick was persuaded to "boost" his first automobile by a gang of local hoodlums (of which he was a member). The group of teenage boys, including Uncle Sam and Grandpa Nick, were determined to have an exciting adventure. Their plan was to travel to Arkansas to meet a group of ladies. One of the boys made a phone call: "She said come on down. She has friends for us all. She's also got some moonshine."

The boys grinned. But one big problem remained: how would the five of them get from downtown St. Louis to Nowhere, Arkansas? That required further contemplation.

The boys had a little money, mostly collected by turning in discarded soda bottles to the local general store. Even pooled together, their resources wouldn't yield enough for bus tickets. The group was too cool to ask their parents for a ride, and what kind of parent would willingly participate in such a calamity?

The answer to their dilemma was parked a block away. "We're gonna take a car!" announced Uncle Sam. Hotwiring this car would be simple. The group knew Grandpa Nick was their best shot at pulling off the heist, but the fleet-footed *dago* needed encouragement. The other four boys set the scene: "The open road, booze, and broads." And just like that, Grandpa Nick was sold.

Grandpa Nick waited until nightfall, while the other four boys waited around the corner in the alleyway. He sneaked up to the driver's side of the four-door Mercury, a 1950 model. Its jet-black paint reflected the glow of the streetlamps. He opened the door and crawled onto the front floorboard. The interior, lacking a ceiling light, was pitch black, so he had to leave the door partially open. As he lay there, trying to locate the right wire, a car approached.

This vehicle looked unique. Grandpa Nick knew its shape meant trouble. A domed light was visible on top: a police squad car. As the car crawled closer, Grandpa Nick remained composed. He sat up quickly in the driver's seat, shut the door, and gripped the wheel, as if he had a right to be there.

The officer drove by, oblivious to the felony in progress. When the coast was clear, he resumed his position on the floorboard. There it was—he'd found the wire. He spliced the hot wire and the wire to the starter. Electric sparks signaled success. The headlights flashed on. Uncle Sam and the others sprinted to their freedom.

The starter cranked and cranked until it finally turned over. A thunderous roar emanated from the exhaust pipe. After the four boys piled in, a yell was heard from the front porch: "What are you doing? Get the fuck out of my car!" screamed the victim. The familiar sound of a shotgun being pumped rang out.

Grandpa Nick mashed the accelerator as the doors slammed shut. The engine revved. The tires screeched, finally gripping the pavement and propelling the boys out of danger. Away they sped, laughing and giggling.

The boys quickly left the bright lights of the city. The difference between the city and the country was stark. Stars sparkled in the night sky, like black construction paper sprinkled with silver and gold glitter. The moon reflected ominously off the car. On they traveled—nothing could stop them now!

Except for an empty gas tank. Their fuel would only get them to Fredericktown, Missouri, a small blip on the map with only one filling station. Fortunately, the station was open all night. Unfortunately, it was frequented by police officers.

As they pulled up to the pump, a gas jockey in a grey jumpsuit stained with grease and mechanical fluid approached the stolen Mercury. "You want her filled up?" he asked. A nod, and the man removed the nozzle from the pump. The boys knew better than to shut the car off while they waited—re-hotwiring it could have drawn suspicion. As the tank filled, the ruffians plotted their next step. The next landmark was Poplar Bluff. Uncle Sam, seated on the passenger side, attempted to confirm. "Po...Po...Po..." he stuttered. The others waited. "Police!" he finally blurted out. The night watchman approached.

"How are you boys doing tonight?" he asked, his tone implying more than just a casual conversation. "Just swell," answered one of the boys. The officer watched the car shake slightly from the rattling of its passengers' nerves. A motorcade of Missouri state highway patrolmen interrupted the conversation. The troopers quickly blocked the exits and encircled the Mercury.

Without incident, the boys were removed from the vehicle, handcuffed, and stuffed into the rear seats of the cruisers. Grandpa and Uncle Sam ended up in the same car, separated from the law by a metal cage. "We followed you all the way from the city," the driver said. The boys believed they had been escaping the confinement of the city, but they had really been traveling straight toward a well-laid trap, a commute to their own incarceration.

Upon arrival at the station, the boys were placed in a holding cell: a typical cell, with cinder block walls and iron bars spaced closely enough to prevent escape. Metal platforms built into the wall served as beds. One wall contained a sink, and next to it was a toilet. One by one, they were removed from their new lodgings and questioned about the crime.

The youngest Randazzo boy went first. Grandpa Nick had learned early on that loose lips sank ships. Randazzos didn't talk to cops. The interrogation began in a friendly tone: "Would you like a smoke?" asked the investigator, oblivious to the fact that he was dealing with a minor. A shake of the head was the only response he'd get during the entire interview.

"What's your name, son?" asked the officer. Silence. "Where'd you get the car?" Silence. Who are your buddies? Where were you boys headed?" he questioned, his anger rising and patience thinning. Silence. "You will answer for this, one way or another," the sleuth snarled, implying physical force. Grandpa Nick's resolve held, knowing the encounter was about to become an assault.

The officer struck Grandpa across the face with an open hand. Nothing. A back-hand slap followed. Nothing. A third blow was dealt. The same response followed. Giving up, the officer ripped Grandpa out of the chair by the cuffs and forced him back into the cell where his confederates were waiting.

Grandpa always paused the story there to interject: "They would have never figured it out if one of them rats hadn't dropped the lip." He always implied that someone had answered the officer's questions. One couldn't blame a youngster for cooperating, but these boys were all Sicilian, all children of men who had been "made." They knew better than to snitch. Putting the pieces together, I suspect competent police work resulted in their identification, unknowing surveillance, and capture.

The story would then pick back up. After each boy was interviewed, they were returned to the holding cell, where they remained for the next four days. They were poorly fed; the jail wasn't manned by dedicated employees, so patrol officers handled the duties normally assigned to a jailer—and only if they had time. The first day there were three meals, each consisting of a baloney sandwich. The second day there were two baloney sandwiches. The third, one. The fourth, only bread. Their maltreatment led to a resolution of defiance. First, they removed the toilet from the floor, flooding the cell. Next, they ripped the sink from the wall, accelerating the flooding. Finally, they tore the bunks from their anchors. The group demolished the cell.

Upon completing their protest, the boys heard a familiar voice. The jailhouse door opened, and the patriarch of the Randazzo family entered. His imposing figure scared the boys more than any actions of the government. As the officer unlocked the cell, my Great-Grandpa Joe spoke: "Get in the car. We're going home."

The arresting agency had finally figured out who these boys were and contacted their parents. Sam and Nick were taken home by their liberator. The authorities, after learning the boys' ages, declined to charge them: four days of hell were enough punishment for their childish actions. The group of miscreants escaped with minor discomfort. Life is littered with failed plans; we should always be thankful when a savior rescues us from their consequences. Soon enough, Grandpa Nick would become a savior himself.

SALT OF THE EARTH

Formal education was never a priority in my family. None of my grandparents ever made it past what we would call elementary school. When they grew up, there was no secondary school in Greenville, Missouri. The one-room schoolhouses of their childhood took them away from the farming work necessary to survival. The land and Jesus would provide everything they needed in this life. These values, hard work and faith, were the basis of the union between my great-grandfather, a lumberjack named Willard Leach, and my great-grandmother, Erva Burchard, a preacher's daughter. Soon after the marriage, Melba Janelle Leach, my paternal grandmother, was born on November 17, 1940, at their home near Greenville. She was followed by two younger sisters, Linda and Faye, and a brother, Ronald.

For some reason, no one ever called her by her first name. "Melba" sounds strange even to me. People mostly called her Janelle—or "Nell," when pronounced with their distinctive southern drawl. I've always known her as Grandma Janelle. Erva ensured her children attended the church pastored by her family, where they learned about God and how to lay life's burdens at the feet of something greater than themselves. The church was where Grandma Janelle learned, and she received some formal education in one of those single-room schoolhouses. Upon reaching her teens, she was forced to work instead of going to school.

When Grandma Janelle was young, her mother was often left to care for the kids while her father worked as a logger. My Great-Grandpa Leach was the last of a generation that did all their logging by hand. Every day, Willard would go to the woods with his axe, handsaw, and mules, returning to the mill with lumber in tow. Erva tended the garden and animals. The family had nothing to their name other than a backwoods cabin, some mules, chickens, and a few dairy cows—but that was enough.

Such a tough existence often compels people to try to escape their reality, either through the bottle or the Bible. Both escapes were used by my grandmother's family. While Erva and her children focused on the Holy Spirit, Willard preferred the distilled kind. During his drinking days, Willard wasn't the man Erva's family had approved of. Early in Janelle's life, her father purchased a large mill in Arkansas and moved his family, removing them from the influence of his in-laws—but not from the influence of moonshine. Both Willard's and Erva's families had been residents of Wayne County since the beginning of Missouri, their roots tracing back to the hills of Virginia and West Virginia. The traditions of distilling moonshine ran deep there, traditions brought by settlers to the frontier that became Missouri.

As Grandma Janelle told it, my Great-Grandfather Willard had an awakening. He was out in the woods one day, drinking heavily, when he was overcome with a divine motivation. He stripped down to his underwear and jumped into the river. When he emerged, his life had changed. This self-baptism inspired him to quit drinking, abandon his valuable commercial mill in Arkansas, and return to the simple existence he'd previously had in Wayne County.

Since he left his logging equipment in Arkansas, Willard was forced to take on a sharecropping agreement. This arrangement was akin to indentured servitude, not far from slavery. He and his family would work for a farmer, using the farmer's land to grow crops. They were entitled to half of the gross profits, but the yields were seldom more than the expenses associated with keeping up the farmland.

Grandma Janelle told me that one year during a drought, Willard sent his children off to pick cotton to supplement the family income. The four children were given meals and a room by the farm at which they worked. Each day, they would wake up before sunrise and set out with a pillowcase. They were instructed to remove any seeds and impurities from the cotton plant before depositing it into their pillowcase. Not long into each day, the children's fingers would start to bleed, pricked by the crop's sharp points.

The long days rarely yielded much profit. Grandma described working hard to fill one pillowcase per day, and the group never filled more than three. She described how measly their pay was, stating that a full pillowcase would earn them about ten cents. On their best days, their sweat and injuries would earn them thirty cents. And yet, while labor law advocates pushed for restrictions on child labor, the Leach children were happy to contribute. I speculate that Willard knew the children were better off "away at the farm," provided with meals, than they were staying home and suffering with him through the tough times.

Decades later, I would visit the backwoods cabin my great-grandfather called home for most of his life. Even in the late 1980s, I was amazed how remote and off-the-grid their homestead was. Driving down D Highway from Greenville towards Wappapello, I could feel the moment when I left my reality behind and entered Grandma Janelle's childhood. The winding roads leading to the lake blurred the distinction between the 1940s and the 1980s. We would always phone ahead to ensure the creek wasn't up, as rain would make the journey impossible. Absent a water barrier, we'd turn off at the Kime General Baptist Church and drive down the dirt road, which was in the worst spot it could have been. Mountains flanked each side, and water puddles were almost always present. The red clay from the mountainsides bled onto the pathway and valley beneath.

To reach the cabin, we had to accelerate quickly up the hillside and turn right into the driveway. The home was about the size of a modern garage, and a small outbuilding sat next to it—an outhouse, since the house had no indoor toiletries. I'm not sure if they couldn't afford a septic system or if the landscape made installing one problematic, but the home didn't get flushing toilets until Ronald Reagan was leaving the White House. The rest of the home was as modest as its bathroom. The cabin had three rooms: a kitchen, a living room, and a bedroom. By the time I came along, the kitchen had received a significant upgrade, a cooking stove powered by natural gas. However, a wood stove remained in the center of the living room, providing much-needed heat.

By the time I knew him, Willard was no longer a logger. He worked year-round to locate, chop, and stack only enough wood to make it through the winter. He hunted and fished all year long. Even in his sixties and seventies, my great-grandfather lived off the land. Six days a week, he stayed active, but Sundays were reserved for church. Grandma Janelle, too, reserved her Sabbath Day for Jesus, and frequently attempted to impress upon me the importance of a day of rest and restoration of the soul. Eventually, Grandma's persistence led me to my own relationship with God.

Most people look for their purpose in life by trying to find a job, meet a mate, and have children. Leaving home at sixteen, Janelle Leach also searched for her purpose in those things. She achieved one of them early in her life. Grandma Janelle's first marriage wasn't discussed by my family—I only recently found out about it by searching online archives for family history. The details are few, but here's what I know: Grandma Janelle married a man who promised her heaven but put her through hell. He would drink, and she would get black eyes.

My grandmother and her abuser moved to St. Louis, where the mistreatment continued. Contrary to the norms of the time, Grandma Janelle was expected to work outside the home to pay the bills so that her husband could get lost in a bottle. The most prominent feature of her personality today is her desire to make people feel comfortable and welcome, so it's no surprise that she worked as a waitress at a corner café in downtown St. Louis. She spent her days taking orders and her nights taking punches—until a certain Sicilian scoundrel convinced her that she deserved to be treated better. Nick Randazzo frequented the café to see her, and he convinced her that he could protect her. So convinced, Janelle left her first husband. Soon after, she was accepted into the Randazzo family, marrying the youngest of their brood and remaining married to him for the next 57 years.

Erva Leach, my great-grandmother, remained married to Willard Leach until she passed away in 1990. My memories of Erva remind me so much of Grandma Janelle. They were sweet and simple women who considered making others happy and spreading the Gospel their primary purposes.

In his later life, however, my great-grandfather became yet another stain upon my family's history. In my family, you always knew something life-changing was happening when people showed up at Grandpa Nick's house and the kids were told to leave. One such occurrence happened in my teens. I don't remember the day, and frankly, I was removed from the conversation, but I remember that Grandma Janelle's siblings showed up unannounced, and then there was a lot of crying. Their father wasn't with them. I suspected Willard had passed away. While that wasn't the case, I would never see him again.

Some time later, I was told that my great-grandfather had been put into a nursing home. It seemed appropriate, given his advanced age, so my lack of suspicion was reasonable. Unbeknownst to me, the nursing home story was a cover for what had really happened. I only discovered the real circumstances of Willard's last few years after stumbling across some information online. Missouri has a criminal case management system that provides information about previous court cases. Even before going to law school, I browsed that database. I'm not sure what prompted me, but I searched all my family members.

There were no real surprises until I searched for Willard Leach. On September 16, 1998, Willard Leach was arrested for attempted forcible rape and statutory sodomy in the first degree. While I don't know the specifics, such charges indicate that he touched the genitals, mouth, or anus of a child less than twelve years of age, or that he forced a child less than twelve years of age to touch his genitals, mouth, or anus for his sexual gratification. Ironically, September 16, 2010, was the day I found out I'd passed the Missouri Bar Exam and would be sworn in as a lawyer.

There wasn't much information to examine; I could only see the charges and the disposition of his case. One charge was dismissed. Willard waived the preliminary hearing on the remaining charge of statutory sodomy in the first degree. There was no record of what happened after that—more digging was necessary. I stumbled upon an article online that contained more details, including a name I recognized. The prosecuting attorney, who is now a colleague, was quoted. The article indicates that the victim was a seven-year-old child.

I vaguely remember a discussion of Willard's mental status at that time. Knowing what I know about the law and the lack of existing records, I suspect that my great-grandfather should have been committed to the state mental hospital, either due to a plea or a motion indicating he lacked the mental capacity to appreciate the wrongfulness of his conduct. But his fate was sealed by a guilty plea, and at 79 years old he was sentenced to 25 years in prison. What few details remain reveal an additional irony: the case was filed in Wayne County, Missouri, and assigned to Division 2 of the Circuit Court. In 2020, I was elected by the people of the 42nd Judicial Circuit of Missouri to serve as the judge of that very division. I now preside over the court that was responsible for the incarceration of my great-grandfather.

I never knew Grandma Janelle's father to be anything but a kind man. He spoke often about his relationship with God, and he took me hunting and fishing. I never observed anything that would have led me to believe he was a pedophile. I see two distinct possibilities. First, that he used his gentle demeanor to gain the trust of his would-be victims. Predators who use these tactics are often referred to as wolves in sheep's clothing, but the comparison isn't fair to wolves, who protect their own young. This is the worst type of offender.

A second possibility is that Willard was truly experiencing a mental decline that caused him to act the way he did. If that's the case, placing him in a facility to ensure those actions didn't happen again was the appropriate response, providing an opportunity for treatment and controlling access to potential victims. However, removing those types of people from familiar settings often exacerbates their issues.

I want to be abundantly clear: I am in no way defending, denying, or condoning his actions. I wasn't old enough to know what happened when it happened. I've never heard the story, from family or otherwise. I know the prosecuting attorney who handled the case, and I find him to be reputable and ethical. I fully expect that whatever Willard was accused of, he did. I assume the argument was made that he had some diminished capacity due to his age and dementia. Regardless, a young child was left victimized, and the person responsible was prevented from victimizing anyone else ever again. Justice was served.

UNANCHORED

My maternal grandmother, Saundra Ann Britt, was born in Galveston, Texas. Grandma Sandy was a foster child, and spent her youth moving from orphanage to orphanage. I know that she lived in Galveston; San Diego, California; and St. Louis, Missouri. I expect that it is hard to settle on a permanent place to live when you don't know where you came from. I wonder how much different her life would have been if she had gotten to know both of her biological parents. She had little memory of her mother, and she worked her whole life to try to forget her father. She requested to be cremated after she died, and so remains unanchored, unattached to some tiny physical space in the graveyard. She is an eternal wanderer.

Grandma Sandy had many remarkable traits, the greatest of which was resilience. She had a cycle with men: find a man, love him, devote herself to him, and then be devastated by him. The cycle started with her father. When his wife died, Robert Britt was left the single father of Grandma Sandy. She was three years old. I often think about when each of my kids was that age. It is worth noting that my stepson, Jacob, came into my life when he was three. While we do not share genetic markers, he is undoubtedly my son. What my grandmother lost at three years old, Jacob had gained. I remember Grandma Sandy telling me that she barely remembered her mother's face, but she could still recall the scent of her perfume, a mix of rose and vanilla.

I only learned of Robert Britt after I received the results of a genetic test. It was a somber but satisfying day going over those results with my Grandma Sandy. I was able to locate some records and even a picture of a young family. The caption read, "Robert, Ruby, and their daughter Saundra." Her eyes lit up when I showed her a picture of her mom and dad. In the picture, that family looked so happy. I often say that I couldn't do it without my wife, Amanda—that I couldn't raise my kids by myself. But even if she weren't around, I would damn sure give it my best effort. I ponder this dilemma more than I should. I remember holding my son Joey, right after he had been born. At that moment, at that very precise second, I knew why I was here. I knew that I would take every ounce of suffering for eternity to let him feel just a fleeting moment of joy. What happened to Robert Britt to make him feel so differently?

Robert Britt was the first bad man in Grandma Sandy's life. As her biological father, he should have been her protector. A special bond is supposed to exist between a father and his daughter. The primary duty of the father is to keep his daughter safe. If the father is a monster, how can he shield his child from the bad in the world? The second directive of the father is to be an example for how his daughter should expect to be treated by all other men in her life.

Based upon the second directive, Robert Britt is responsible for the cycle of exploitation Grandma Sandy found herself in. Not until she was a great-grandmother did she break it. Not until she found Ron Angel—but that story is yet to come.

After Grandma Sandy's mother died, she was left with her father. Britt forced her, as she grew, to take on the roles her mother had served. He made her his housekeeper, responsible for cooking and cleaning. Later, he made her his sexual partner. The easiest parts of her life were the times when she was too busy to be used for sex. Housework gave her temporary reprieve from her father's sexual advances. Eventually, Grandma Sandy realized that her situation was not normal. That realization left her with a decision to make. She could tell someone who could help, and be taken away from all she had ever known; or she could remain silent, and continue to be Britt's slave in all aspects of her life.

Disclosure it was. The decision to tell the story of how one was violated carries a tremendous weight. Sometimes that decision must be made by a child. Before she was a teen, Grandma Sandy had to make such a decision, and would have to accept the full gravity of it for the remainder of her life. She knew that telling the authorities what happened to her meant she would instantly be made an orphan—but having nothing in life is better than being a perpetual victim. Upon disclosure, Grandma Sandy was removed from her father by child protective services. She was taken to an orphanage, where her life of nothingness would begin. There, she hoped that a new family would adopt her, a family that actually wanted her. A family that loved her. That family never came. Upon reaching the age of sixteen, Sandy was ejected from the orphanage and left to fend for herself in the world, a world that was harsh to an unprotected, helpless, and homeless drifter.

She became a vagrant. Homelessness brought the challenge of finding somewhere to get out of the elements. She tried to avoid places that were rainy or too hot to be outside during the day. She avoided cold places where the thought of her freezing crept in during long winter nights.

Grandma Sandy wandered around the country as a young woman. At some point, she ended up in San Diego,

California. I would guess that it could be a fine landing spot for a nomad: great weather, the beach, and many single servicemembers looking for young women to love. It was there that Grandma Sandy would meet the next man in her cycle.

The word "bud" usually brings to mind a certain friendliness. Slap "grandpa" in front of it, and you picture a jolly old man—gray hair, twinkling eyes, maybe a chuckle or two. That's not who I got. While he was, technically, my grandpa, we were never buds.

Bud—born Benjamin Franklin Finlay Jr.—came from a family with a peculiar sense of tradition. His parents, Benjamin Sr. and Christine Mary Litteken, stuck so closely to the family script that their two kids ended up as Benjamin and Christine, too. I never met my great-grandfather, Ben. His wife—who I called Grandma Chris—I knew well. She had survived the Great Depression—and wouldn't let anyone forget it. She lived in St. Louis her whole life, and though you wouldn't peg her for the outdoorsy type, every memory I have of her involves a walk in the woods, or her whipping up some wild plant we'd found into something delicious to eat. She saved everything. Her house was a maze, a living monument to the idea that someone's trash is another's treasure. She hoarded because she had known true scarcity. She outlived her husband and her child. Surviving was the consolation prize for her hard-fought life. I still can't believe that my grandfather, a man filled with darkness, came from that gentle, resourceful woman.

Bud grew up in St. Louis with his parents and his sister. I wish I could say I knew more about his life, but he died in 1991, and my memories of him are all from the end: bald, frail, and fighting lung cancer. People tell me I look like him, but, thankfully, that resemblance is all I inherited. Cancer took him, and for that, I'm not sure I don't owe cancer a debt.

Bud was a successful businessman, and made most of his money in real estate. I remember stopping at construction sites he owned while tagging along with my mom as she drove him to chemo appointments. I was too small to help, but when they were younger, my mother and her sisters weren't so lucky. During their time with Bud, they weren't family—they were laborers. As they grew up, their labor took on a more sinister shape. Bud would invite men over, offer them a private room, and then offer them one of his daughters.

Stinginess defined Bud, both in life and in death. I hated the ritual of visiting him as a kid. His house always smelled of pie, candy, and soda, but he guarded those treats like gold. I remember asking for just a bite of lemon meringue pie or a sip of soda and being told no, every time. It's hard to see the best in a man who won't share a sliver of pie with his grandson. Somehow, he was even meaner with his possessions in death. He left behind property, real estate, equipment—but locked it all away from his daughters, his wife, and his grandchildren.

Military service is supposed to build virtue. Bud got the hero's funeral at Jefferson Barracks National Cemetery, but he was not worthy of the honor. To the families of the real heroes buried there, I'm sorry. We rarely speak of Grandpa Bud. There are secrets, old and heavy, that my mother and her sisters hoped would finally be buried with him. But trauma like that never stays buried for long. Eventually, the river overflows its banks, flooding whatever peace you managed to build.

Benjamin Franklin Finlay Jr., a good-looking Navy man, wooed my Grandma Sandy. He was stationed in San Diego, but he lived halfway across the country in the then-thriving Midwest city of St. Louis. Bud and Grandma Sandy were so enthralled with each other that they were married right there in San Diego. Bud was looking for companionship, and Sandy was searching for stability and protection. Temporarily, each would be satisfied with the other. Bud Finlay finished his military commitment and returned home with his bride. Like a devoted partner was expected to, Grandma Sandy packed up. She was ready to follow Grandpa Bud to the end of the earth, but they planted roots in St. Louis. This permanent settlement marked a first for Grandma Sandy, and St. Louis would be her home for the rest of her life.

Not long after arriving in St. Louis, Grandpa Bud and Grandma Sandy started having children. First, Ronda, then Lisa, and last, my mom, Barbera. Grandma Sandy gave birth to three little girls in four years. She was satisfied with her progeny, but Grandpa Bud still wanted a son to whom he could pass on his name and his business acumen. He believed that women should not inherit property. They should not participate in the workforce. They should be subservient to their spouses. They should remain home to tend to the house and take care of the kids. A man was responsible for filling his own cup, and the women got whatever he did not drink. Bud treated his wife and daughters very poorly, and his misogyny caused a rift within their family: he began to view Sandy as his property and her daughters as his burden. In his opinion, the failure to produce an heir was entirely the fault of his wife. He was so ashamed of his sonless family that he gave the girls nicknames: Ron, Lee, and Bob. Eventually, he forced Grandma and the girls to leave the home. Grandma Sandy was left with three little girls, no husband, no job, and no hope.

Deprived of her home and marriage, Grandma Sandy was determined to take care of her girls herself. She was newly single, in an unfamiliar city, with three young children who fully depended upon her for their sustenance. Her headstrong nature and independence spurred her to take on two jobs. Many days and nights, Ronda was left in charge of her two younger siblings. Chaos was a continual presence in their lives.

Eventually, Grandma Sandy moved on to the next man in her cycle. This relationship is one of the many family secrets that I just don't have a whole lot of details about. I can only regurgitate what I think I know. I have never talked openly to anyone who lived through it, but I have heard my mom, aunts, and Grandma Sandy slip up and reveal little bits while I was listening—sometimes surreptitiously.

Aunt Ronda, Aunt Lisa, and my mom were each molested as children and teens. None of the sisters were aware it was happening to the others. My grandma was not aware it was happening to any of her kids. I do not place blame on her, but the perpetrators were men that she trusted, allowed into her home, and permitted to be around her girls while she was working multiple jobs trying to make ends meet. I often wonder what life would have been like had she met the right man when her girls were still little. How different would their lives have been?

Grandma Sandy was highly intelligent. She started working at McDonald-Douglas, a company that would eventually be bought out by Boeing, as a production worker, spending her days assembling minor parts of airplanes. Her dedication to her job earned her many promotions and transfers to other positions. She worked her way to the role of design engineer, responsible for designing and improving portions of jets and rockets. Grandma Sandy was, quite literally, a rocket scientist.

Boeing would also bring into her life her final husband. Ron Angel worked with Grandma Sandy for years. What started out as a platonic work relationship ended with me getting a Grandpa Ron. This Ron was different. He was a good, moral man.

I believe that finding out who her mother was broke Grandma Sandy's cycle of being devastated by men, and helped her find the right type of mate to be her final husband. I am glad that the cycle ended with Grandpa Ron, with whom she remained happily married until she passed away from cancer. It took her a lifetime to find the right man, but in the end, she did—even as she lay suffering in her last moments of life, Ron never deserted her. I only wish that she had had more life to spend with him. Grandma Sandy's life taught me the enduring strength of the human spirit. She may have been unanchored in life, but her legacy will forever be etched in my heart.

THE WEIGHT OF INNOCENCE

Trigger Warning: This chapter contains graphic
content related to sexual assault and trauma.

Life has never been easy for my mother. Barb was born the youngest of Sandy and Bud's three girls. She always had beautiful blonde hair, and her beauty still shines today. What many view as a gift, however, has been a lifelong curse for my mother. Although her looks earned her much attention and praise throughout her life, some of it came from dangerous adult men, and when she was at a vulnerable age.

My mom was sexually assaulted as a child by an adult male that Grandma Sandy had taken as her second husband. This victimization as a teenager would eventually split up the relationship, and the perpetrator would be long gone before I was old enough to meet him. On the outside, he appeared to be a good guy, but he was the worst type of predator. Our family does not talk about this. My mom doesn't talk about this. It feels like I am betraying some type of blood oath by writing about it. Nevertheless, this event was part of the darkness and chaos that existed in her childhood.

While it is an extremely unfortunate coincidence, Grandma Sandy's second and third husbands had the same first name—but that was all they had in common. Ron number one entered Grandma Sandy's life under the illusion that he would be her savior. He was attractive and charismatic, and he provided relief from my grandma's dire financial circumstances. Like most sexual predators, he was able to convince his unsuspecting victim he was harmless.

Even more despicably, the man would eventually admit to his wrongdoing—but he shamed and blamed my mother. He tried to justify his actions based on the way she dressed. He insisted that his victim wanted the abuse to happen.

When this abuse was disclosed, Grandma Sandy went into survival mode. She isolated her girls from the man. Once she was convinced they were out of harm's reach, she went to the police for their assistance. The police wanted to speak with the victim. Even today, a victim's disclosures of sexual abuse are viewed with a great deal of skepticism. In the late 1970s and early 1980s, they were viewed with much more than that. Mom's account was met with outright denial.

Relaying the details of any victimization can be traumatic. Being forced to do so as a child is borderline inhumane. Police officers should approach investigations as objective, fact-finding historians. When a disclosure is made, they should use their investigation to corroborate or dispute the information they are provided. But what happened to my mother is not acceptable in any investigation. Instead of gathering her testimony to assist in the investigation of a horrendous crime, an officer essentially interrogated my mother about why she would lie to get a good man in trouble. She was forced to give intimate details of each encounter. She was forced to find evidence that corroborated her story. Most inappropriately, she was forced to take a polygraph examination.

Polygraph tests are administered by a professional who is supposed to be trained in the usage of the polygraph device, delivery of the test, and analysis of the results. They attach to the subject sensors that can register bodily reactions, like changes in heart rate, pulse rate, blood pressure, respiration, and skin conductivity. The subject is then asked specific questions, and the device's measurements are alleged to indicate whether or not they're lying.

Before the agency would proceed with requesting charges be filed against Ron, Mom would have to take a polygraph examination. This was over 40 years ago. Technology and the standards for using it have evolved over the past four decades; today, it is not just discouraged, but outright illegal to force a victim to take a polygraph examination. Additionally, modern research indicates that these tests are highly inaccurate. Even more importantly, research suggests that victims have different physiological responses than perpetrators, making even a well-meaning examiner liable to misinterpret the results in an unusual case like my mother's.

Knowing all this, it is not surprising that Barb was deemed to have failed the polygraph examination. That test almost ended the investigation. Had it have not been for my grandmother's steadfast pursuit of protection for her daughter, the sexual abuse allegations would have been dismissed as unfounded.

At first, Ron had denied that he had molested my mother. But, convinced that my mom was telling the truth, Grandma Sandy continued to seek justice. When the man was subjected to another interview, Grandma Sandy was the interrogator.

"She is not backing down from her story," she explained to Ron. "Why would she keep saying you did this to her? Are you sure nothing happened between the two of you? She's not your daughter. Maybe she was being flirty with you, and she really wanted it to happen?" Sandy posed these leading questions with the expertise of a detective, and the suspect's affect began to change.

"She's… she's a cheerleader. She is always dressing up in those skimpy outfits and dancing around. I can't believe she acts that way," Ron replied. He continued his attempts to obviate his responsibility for what occurred: "She knew what she was doing. I could tell she wanted it to happen." The cracks developing in his story exposed him to further questioning. "What do you mean? She wanted what? You think that a fourteen-year-old girl wanted her first experience to be with you?" asked Sandy.

Ron broke down. "Yes," he admitted. "She was seeking attention from me that she couldn't get elsewhere. You can only be teased so much before you give in to those temptations." That was enough for Grandma Sandy. She returned to the station to share Ron's confession with the lead detective. After confirming that Barb and Sandy were willing to testify, the officer finally agreed that there was enough evidence to file the case.

Charges were filed, Ron was arrested, and a trial was set—but Barb would never get her chance at justice. Ron was granted an undeserved escape from prosecution and the life of confinement that would surely follow: before the case could proceed to trial, he died of a heart attack. For this type of man and this type of case, it was a fate more generous than prison. It saved him from having to face his accuser, from receiving a formal conviction, and from suffering the wrath of the punitive sword belonging to Lady Justice.

Life never gave Mom anything but her good looks and resilience. Most of her life, all she wished for was adequacy. At times, she was provided no more by her single mother than a roof over her head and enough food to sustain her. But although her wardrobe consisted only of hand-me-downs and the occasional thrift store purchase, her beauty still shined. She hoped to find someone who could rescue her from her circumstances, from the basement of her mind where she was held captive by her victimization. Mom spent her entire childhood trying to be loved.

Her family moved from place to place during her upbringing, but never strayed far from the St. Louis area. Grandma Sandy did her best to allow her girls to remain close enough to Grandpa Bud that he could be present in their lives. But unless he "needed" the girls for something, he never took advantage of this opportunity.

The abuse from Ron had ended, but my mom's troubles were only just beginning. The trauma she still suffered from led to addictions to drugs and alcohol. Eventually, she attempted to take her own life. The abuse from Ron and other men who had placed their desire above their virtue had caused my mother untold hurt, and Grandma Sandy was forced to make a difficult decision. She decided to commit Mom, at sixteen, to a psychiatric facility. A psychiatric hospital is supposed to be a place where lost souls are reunited with their minds and bodies, but a portion of my mom's soul and innocence was lost there. She told me, once, in detail, what had happened there.

She will never forget the smell. At first, the lemon bleach clinical prophylactic smelled of hope and change for her—but in her memory that scent will forever be attached to fear, despair, and victimization. "How did I get here?" she wondered. She lay staring at the ceiling as she flipped through her mental photo album of trauma. The first picture was of her best friend, Susie.

Susie was her confidant. She would listen as Barb discussed the multiple instances of sexual assault she had suffered. Mom had been a sounding board for Susie, as well. Susie told of the unhappiness in her own life. While Mom knew that Susie's mental health was suspect, she didn't imagine that Suzie would harm herself—but as an alternative to facing further mental anguish, Suzie ended her own life. Barb felt abandoned by her best friend.

Before she could turn that page in her mind, her peripheral vision alerted her to motion near the doorway. Dismissing it as normal hallway traffic, and expecting the door to be securely locked, she attempted to return to her thoughts. But a slow creaking drew her attention back to the doorway. Inch by inch, more of the hallway became visible. Finally, a small amount of light revealed a shadowy figure standing before her bed. She could not recognize the outline in the poor lighting, and just as she discerned that the figure wasn't her nurse, the door slammed shut.

Standing in her room was a man who worked at the facility, fully dressed in a hospital employee's uniform. Brain signals travel very quickly, but Barb's brain could not warn her fast enough to yell for help. The man quickly sprang toward the bed. He placed one hand firmly over her mouth and brandished a sharp metal object in the other. Barb could feel the warmth of his rank breath on her face as he panted. "Don't say a word, or I'll kill you," the man whispered into her ear. Barb lay still as he manhandled her body. After slinging her legs apart, he ripped aside her medical gown.

Helplessness. Barb knew this feeling. Her mind had felt this type of ultimate defenselessness before. The man completed his vile act and disappeared. Barb lay crying in her bed, and wondered, "Are the pieces of my life worth putting back together?"

For years, Barb never told a soul about what had happened in the facility. For some time after her release from treatment, keeping this trauma bottled up made it hard for her to put the bottle down. She would remain at this rock bottom for a long time.

THE MAKING OF NICKY
Addiction, Violence, and the Search for Control

My dad is an addict, plain and simple. He's addicted to the things that make him feel good: the thrill of the chase, the power of money, the fleeting comfort of women, and the oblivion of substances. It's a constant cycle of seeking pleasure to quiet the demons in his head. I don't excuse his actions, but I understand the compulsions that drive them. His love for me? I know it's there, buried beneath layers of addiction, but his ability to show it is often lost in translation. I've become an expert in reading between the lines, anticipating his shortcomings, and loving him not for what he could be, but for the flawed, complicated man he actually is.

Dominick Randazzo Jr., born October 21, 1966, entered the world as the cherished only child of Dominick Sr. and Melba "Janelle" Randazzo (Leach). Affectionately known as "Nicky" or "Little Nicky," he bore the weight of his family's expectations. While his name spoke to his Italian heritage, his appearance told a different story. With thin blond hair and pale skin, Nicky was a Leach through and through, a stark contrast to the dark-haired, olive-skinned Randazzos. He remained lean and wiry throughout his life, and his beanpole build made him an easy target for bullies in the rough-and-tumble environment of 1970s Jennings, Missouri.

Growing up in Jennings, a working-class suburb of St. Louis, wasn't always easy. The city, still grappling with the social and economic changes of the era, had its share of challenges. Factories were closing, unemployment was rising, and a sense of unease hung in the air. For Nicky, the playground became a microcosm of this larger world, a place where he had to learn to defend himself against those who saw him as an easy mark.

The first time Nicky came home with a black eye, Grandpa Nick didn't offer sympathy. Instead, he delivered a brutal lesson that would forever shape Nicky's approach to conflict. "Son," he said, his voice hard, "don't let anyone lay a hand on you. If they run their mouth, you hit them first. Get the first lick in. There are no rules in fighting. The goal is to inflict more pain on them than they do on you. Never give up. If they're bigger than you, don't back down. Bite 'em, pinch 'em, poke their eyes. If that don't work, pick something up and hit them with it."

Those words, echoing the brutal pragmatism of his own grandfather, Joe—a man rumored to have ties to La Cosa Nostra—transformed Nicky. He became a problem looking for an answer, a rabid dog eager to attack. Grandpa Nick had inadvertently created a monster. Nicky no longer fought out of necessity—he fought because he craved the adrenaline, the chaos, the feeling of control.

Adding fuel to the fire was the spoiling he received as an only child. His parents, particularly his mother, Janelle, indulged his every whim. He learned to manipulate them, to use his intelligence and silver tongue to get what he wanted, regardless of the consequences. This sense of entitlement, coupled with his growing penchant for violence, created a volatile mix.

For much of Nicky's childhood, Grandpa Nick worked as a truck driver, spending weeks on the road. With Grandpa Nick gone, Janelle, used to deferring to her husband's authority, struggled to discipline Nicky. In the father's absence, a simmering resentment grew between mother and son. Each vying for Grandpa Nick's attention, they would eagerly snitch on each other upon his return, painting the other in the worst possible light.

Eventually, Grandpa Nick left trucking behind, unaware that fate would soon lead him back to the open road. He and his brother, Sam, decided to open a business together: Sand Dunes Buggy Shop. As the name suggested, they manufactured, sold, and repaired buggies, specializing in rail buggies—stripped-down machines with exposed frames, offering a thrilling, if dangerous, driving experience.

In the late 1970s and early 1980s, these contraptions were surprisingly popular, and the business thrived. Flush with cash, Grandpa Nick continued to spoil Nicky, showering him with gifts and further reinforcing his sense of entitlement.

Nicky, in turn, honed his skills in manipulation and violence. Alcohol became a catalyst for his aggression, stripping away any semblance of restraint. Whether it was finishing another bottle or finishing an opponent, Nicky never knew when to stop. He was, by all accounts, a nasty drunk. He took fights beyond their normal bounds, aiming to disable his opponents, to teach them a lesson. One such lesson would land him in the crosshairs of a dangerous man.

Some motorcycle clubs refer to themselves as "one-percenters." The figure refers to the belief that ninety-nine percent of bikers are law-abiding citizens. The man known as "Shooter," the leader of a local biker gang and a notorious hit man, fell into that small percentage who proudly touted their illicit actions. Within the unforgiving world of these outlaws, Shooter was not someone to be trifled with.

At sixteen, Nicky was still a scrawny kid, but he possessed a reckless bravado that belied his size. Always on the lookout for excitement, he stumbled into a confrontation with Shooter's brother. The details of the initial altercation are hazy, lost to time and embellished retellings, but the end result was undeniable: a brutal, no-holds-barred brawl that spilled across Shooter's front yard.

Nicky, fueled by adrenaline and a thirst for chaos, fought with a ferocity that surprised everyone—even himself. The fight became a whirlwind of fists, feet, and broken landscaping. Bushes were uprooted, mulch was scattered, and the lion statues guarding the front porch were shattered. The violence escalated, culminating in the two combatants crashing through the windshield of a parked luxury car, turning the interior into a blood-soaked mess.

In the end, Nicky emerged victorious, leaving Shooter's brother battered and broken in the intensive care unit. Nicky, sporting his own share of bruises and broken bones, walked away with a twisted sense of pride.

But his victory came at a price. When Shooter learned of his brother's fate, he flew into a rage. Fueled by vengeance, he grabbed a shotgun and set out to find Nick Randazzo.

Shooter arrived at the Randazzo home, intent on delivering a fatal dose of retribution. He pounded on the door, shotgun in hand, and confronted Grandpa Nick. "Are you Nick Randazzo? Did you hurt my brother?" he snarled, his voice trembling with rage. "Someone is going to pay. You'd better talk."

Grandpa Nick, bewildered and unaware of the day's events, denied any involvement. From his room on the second floor, where he'd been hiding out since the altercation, Nicky overheard the commotion and grabbed his father's 30.06 Remington deer rifle. Sneaking out the back door, he crept up behind Shooter and pressed the barrel of the rifle into the man's back.

"Put down the gun, motherfucker!" Nicky screamed, his voice surprisingly steady despite the terror churning in his gut. A tense standoff ensued. Nicky, shirtless and bloodied, tried to explain the situation, revealing his role in the earlier brawl.

Shooter, his eyes narrowed, surveyed the skinny, wounded teenager before him. "YOU did THAT to my brother?" he asked, disbelief lacing his voice. But the evidence of Nicky's violence was undeniable.

As the sirens of approaching police cars filled the air, the standoff reached its climax. Cooler heads prevailed, and both men reluctantly lowered their weapons. Shooter, shaking his head in disbelief at the sight of the slightly-built boy who had inflicted so much damage, was arrested.

Nicky, thanks to his quick thinking and a healthy dose of luck, avoided legal repercussions. He had once again proved his willingness to confront danger head-on, solidifying his reputation as a force to be reckoned with.

For his sixteenth birthday, he received a 1968 Chevrolet Camaro, a gift facilitated by his great-grandmother Rose, who used her meager savings to buy the dilapidated vehicle. Grandpa Nick used his mechanical skills to transform the rusty shell into a gleaming, candy-apple red race car, complete with a powerful engine, leather interior, and chrome wheels. The freedom of having his own car only amplified Nicky's penchant for trouble.

With his newfound mobility, Nicky expanded his search for excitement beyond the familiar streets of Jennings. He neglected his studies, preferring the thrill of parties and the attention of girls. He was a social butterfly, the envy of every boy in town. But beneath the surface, he was a powder keg waiting to explode.

At sixteen, Nicky craved the party scene, drawn to the allure of alcohol, drugs, and easy conquests. He was a star football player, and the perks of his status included invitations to exclusive parties where he was treated like a celebrity. Cheerleaders lined up for a chance to impress him, and Nicky, never one to shy away from attention, played the part, enjoying the fleeting validation before discarding them.

One such admirer was Gina. She and Nicky were a serious couple, bound together by a reciprocal lust that they mistook for love. At sixteen, it was easy to confuse the two. They quickly married and moved in together. Nicky and Gina fought constantly, their relationship a volatile mix of passion and animosity. The breaking point came when Grandma Janelle had to physically restrain Gina during a particularly violent argument, allowing Nicky to escape the house in nothing but his underwear and combat injuries. When he returned to his parents' home, his relationship with Gina was in ruins.

The events of Nicky's early life—the violence, the addiction, the dysfunctional relationships—laid the foundation for the man he would become: a man driven by a relentless need for control, a man forever searching for something to fill the void within him.

NICKY'S DESCENT INTO CHAOS

My ancestors on Grandpa Randazzo's side were deeply intertwined with the upper echelons of organized crime. The Vitales were from that upper echelon. John Vitale was a "capo," a boss of bosses. Sitting atop the pyramid, he commanded the entire organization. Nicky's inability to control his temper almost ignited a full-blown war within the St. Louis underworld.

Jim Vitale, the mob boss's grandson, and Nicky Randazzo were constantly fighting over Gina. Jim was a formidable opponent, a Golden Gloves champion boxer who could both deliver and absorb considerable punishment. While Vitale honed his skills in the gym, Nicky's training came from the streets. Spectators knew that a clash between these two styles would be worth watching.

The last time they faced off, the "family" intervened. This final confrontation took place at the Randazzo house. For once, Nicky wasn't seeking trouble, but it arrived at his doorstep nonetheless. Gina had a knack for provoking both sides. Antagonizing men like Jim Vitale and the young Nicky Randazzo was easy; tranquility wasn't a part of their nature.

Accompanied by his own crew, Vitale traveled to Jennings to confront Nicky at his home. Never one to back down,

Nicky met Jim on the front lawn. The ensuing fight was the drawn-out bloodbath everyone expected. Only the arrival of the police prevented a decisive outcome.

At the police station, Nicky was familiar with the routine. The cops would ask for his personal information, and upon learning he was sixteen, they'd call his parents. His dad would usually come to the rescue, and he'd end the night back in his own bed. This time, however, Grandma Janelle was summoned. She had far less control over Nicky.

Grandma arrived at the station to be greeted by a group of exasperated police officers. They explained that Nicky was treating his arrest like nothing more than a minor inconvenience. Jim was also at the station, but as he was older, his release wouldn't be so swift. Although separated by bars, the two boys continued their sparring verbally. Grandma could hear them trading insults across the hallway. Just before his release, Nicky managed one last dig: "I'm going to beat your ass next time I see you! I don't care when! I don't care where!" Nicky walked out a free man, leaving his opponent behind bars, but his freedom wouldn't last.

As he and Grandma Janelle exited the police station, they were met by Jim Vitale's mother and sister. The daughter-in-law of John Vitale knew Nicky Randazzo because of the constant fights with her son, and was well aware of his reputation. In the familiar style of an Italian mother, she unleashed her disapproval and disdain on Nicky, exclaiming, "You're a little fucking punk! You've got one coming!"

The threat sparked a reaction from the uncontrollable sixteen-year-old. Nicky decided to be proactive. Right there in the station's entryway, he open-hand slapped Jim Vitale's mother. "Take that, bitch! Now I really got one coming," he taunted with an evil smirk. The Vitale sister, enraged by the sight of her mother being struck, began to berate Nicky, and she suffered the same fate. With handprints across their faces, the Vitales re-entered the station to report the assault. Unfortunately for Nicky, the handprints matched his own hand almost exactly, and the incident was caught on video.

After hitting the Vitale women, Nicky lingered in the parking lot. Two female officers exited the jail and quickly approached Nicky. They calmly greeted the young man, who appeared disheveled and anxious. One of the officers cautiously asked Dad if he was alright. His response: "Arrest that crazy bitch." Nicky's word choice evidently struck a nerve with the officers, and they abruptly ended the discussion. They had already been informed about what had happened to the mafioso's wife and daughter, who were crying inside the police station, and they would soon make Nicky pay for his transgressions. They knew it was time for an attitude adjustment.

Gender roles were more defined in the 1980s than they are today. Many professions had barriers to entry for women, and law enforcement was among the most challenging for women to break into. The two women Nicky had to deal with that day were a minority in the male-dominated trade. As pioneers, they had to prove themselves to many men. They certainly proved themselves to my dad.

Nicky was going to leave the encounter in handcuffs one way or another, but he decided to challenge the women. As Officer 1 announced that he was under arrest, Officer 2 reached for Nicky's arm. He quickly pulled away and attempted to escape apprehension, but Officer 1 blocked his exit. Idiotically, Nicky demanded, "Move, bitch!"

That statement sealed his fate. Dealing with misogyny was these officers' specialty. Officer 1 was armed with a blackjack, a heavy leather pouch about twelve inches long, worn and creased like an old couch. Officer 2 pulled her billy club, a shiny, black, wooden baton. Both women were competent with their weapons.

They began to beat Nicky into compliance. Officer 1 struck repeatedly on one side as Officer 2 pounded away at the other. Nicky responded with continued verbal abuse and further attempts to escape. Eventually, Nicky's will to be free proved weaker than the officers' determination to apprehend him.

Now cuffed and stuffed into the squad car, Nicky's verbal abuse continued. Here, as in most areas of his life, his inability to discern his best interest led to suffering. As they drove away from the police station, the barrage of insults continued. If vulgar words were associated with physical injury, Nick would surely have won the fight—but the women were unfazed.

The cruiser turned an unexpected corner and decelerated. Nicky became less concerned with insults and more concerned about their destination. The vehicle crept into an isolated portion of the town, noticeably absent of streetlights.

After the paddy wagon stopped, the front seat occupants circled to the door nearest their vocal critic. The door remained shut while Nicky heard whispers from the outside. He wondered where they were and why they had settled at this location. He soon learned the answers. The door swung open, and soon after the distinct sound of flesh being struck by the leather-wrapped lead plate—"thwack, thwack, thwack"—echoed through the night. Nicky was beaten mercilessly.

Out of sight of any onlookers, the women took turns tuning up the young ruffian. As soon as the frequency of the strikes slowed, Nicky would bark some insult. In response, the assault would resume. Finally, his will was broken, and the officers discontinued the punishment. Objective fulfilled, they helped him back into the car and returned to the precinct.

When they arrived at their destination, what was once defiance was replaced by compliance. Nicky answered the officers' questions one by one. When asked for his date of birth, Dad replied "October 21, 1966." "1966?" questioned Officer 1. "Yes, ma'am," he replied.

A confused look appeared on each of the officers' faces. "You said you were married," Officer 2 replied. "I am," Nicky replied in a subdued tone. "But you're only sixteen," Officer 2 countered. The women demanded a phone number for his parents. Realizing that they were dealing with a juvenile, the women attempted to rapidly erase the evidence of their gaffe. Soon, Grandpa Nick would be at the station to absolve his son of responsibility.

With a newfound respect for the toughness of two specific female officers, Nicky returned to his parents' house. Despite his behavior with women being corrected and his age saving him twice from lengthy incarceration, it didn't sink in how fortunate he had been. He has told me this story many times, and his explanation for the incident is always misplaced. "Those women cops gave me the worst beating I've ever had. There was not a spot from head to toe that didn't have a bruise. My whole body hurt, and every place I touched made me wince in pain." He blamed the officers' response on their domineering nature and not on his disrespectful actions.

This reckless act of violence against the Vitale women sent shockwaves through the St. Louis Mafia. The Vitales vowed that Nicky wouldn't live to see the end of the week. Capo John Vitale issued a "hit" on Nicky Randazzo for his disrespect and disregard for the hierarchy. In the mafia, a hit meant certain death.

Grandpa Nick received a call from his Uncle Mike, who had learned of Nicky's transgression. He expressed his disapproval, but, at the urging of his sister Rose, agreed to try and get the hit called off. He vouched for Grandpa Nick and Dad, assuring the mob bosses that Nicky was sorry and that the feud between the young Randazzo and Vitale was over.

Uncle Mike reported back to Grandpa Nick, "Little Nicky is out of control. John is unhappy. What was he thinking, hitting a couple of girls? This is the last time I step in to save him." Grandpa Nick assured John Vitale that there was no bad blood between the families and that he would handle his own son. The names and relationships they discussed fostered a mutual respect. An all-out mob war was likely averted that day. Grandpa's people would have retaliated, and the conflict would have escalated. While a full-blown war was avoided, at the hands of those women officers, Nicky had still received the punishment he deserved.

THE ST. VALENTINE'S DAY MASSACRE

Barb Finlay knew of Nicky Randazzo. The groups that the two ran in had some overlap. She knew of Nicky's reputation, his charm, and his volatile temper. Deep down, I think she was looking for a dangerous man. Not the type of dangerous that causes a man to hide his true character; she was looking for the kind of dangerous that a man wears on his sleeve. The kind of dangerous that keeps other people honest in their intentions. Nicky, for her, was like a nuclear arsenal—a promise of mutually assured destruction for anyone who wished her harm.

Their mutual interest in each other was sparked at a party they both had happened to attend. Barb had drunk too much alcohol and passed out. Nicky overheard a conversation about a girl unconscious in the bedroom. A circle of guys discussed the prospect of a non-consensual encounter with the incapacitated girl. In what was truly an act of chivalry, the hero known as Nicky Randazzo swooped in and saved her from another deviant sexual encounter. As the men entered the room where Barb lay unconscious, Nicky followed behind. Once inside, Nicky exploded with his usual rage on the would-be rapists. He gathered up Barb, placed her in the backseat of his car, and drove her home.

This act of chivalry had consequences for the relationship between Nicky and Gina. Ultimately, the death of the toxic relationship between the two resulted in the birth of the relationship between Mom and Dad. The two would eventually agree to escape the chaos of both of their lives in St. Louis for a simpler place—a place called Arcadia. A place where Nicky would ask for her hand in marriage, Barb would get pregnant, and they would start their own family as young parents. But not before one major holiday debacle almost permanently separated Nicky from the free world. One fateful night in February, around the day that many couples celebrate love, he was responsible for a massacre, an event reminiscent of the original that bears its name.

It began like most other nights for Nicky. He waited to hear where the parties were, and then devised his plan for the night. Loaded with three friends, Nicky's Camaro transported the group behind enemy lines to a party in another town. I assume at that point he was just following the crowd, regardless of how hostile the surrounding territory was.

It took extraordinarily little to set him off—a glance, a snarl, or an accidental bump could start a chain of events that changed lives. This night, it was even less. The roar of the Camaro's loud exhaust drowned out the music playing at a home near where he'd parked. Soon after Nicky and his friends exited the car, a group emptied out of the house to see what had interrupted their tunes. Nicky felt threatened by the inquisitive group. He was drunk, and, like clockwork, he got angry. Nicky yelled, "Do you got a problem?" Apparently, they did. In what can only be described as carnage, Nicky began to annihilate anything within striking distance.

As the riot began, it quickly became apparent that Nicky's group was outnumbered. The swarm of partygoers proceeded toward the boys like a mob of zombies, backing them against Nicky's Camaro. Left with little chance to escape, the boys needed an equalizer—and they found one. Crowbars are sometimes associated with burglars, but they're most frequently used in the construction trade to separate materials or remove nails. Nicky imagined a different usage for the one he pulled out of the backseat of his car.

The weapon gave Nicky a divine feeling; like Thor wielding his mighty hammer Mjolnir, he unleashed his rage. He systematically dispatched every buzzing member of the swarm. At the end of it all, he stood over a wasteland of the incapacitated bodies of his victims.

Each of those victims earned him a charge of armed assault with a deadly weapon, with the charge of causing or attempting to cause serious physical injury or death to boot. Upon his arrest, he found himself in familiar territory. He overheard the detective exclaim, "They're not sure the one kid is going to make it," and he knew he was referring to one of the victims. The man whose voice he heard in the hallway entered the room with a stern affect.

Seated on the opposite side of the table, the detective quickly read the suspect his Miranda rights. "You have a right to remain silent. Anything you say can be used against you in a court of law. You have the right to have an attorney present while being questioned. If you cannot afford one, one can be appointed for you. If you begin questioning without an attorney, you can stop answering questions at any time. Do you understand the rights as I've read them to you?"

Nicky nodded. The detective began with an open-ended question: "What happened tonight?" A long, awkward pause ensued. Dad tried as hard as he could, but he didn't remember specifically what had happened. He knew he was at a party and that there was a fight, but all the details in between were a blur. Finally, all he could muster was, "I don't know." He truly didn't.

Normal people don't understand what he meant by that. When he said he blacked out, he meant he had no control over his actions and no recollection of the events. Unfortunately, I can relate. I have experienced the phenomenon myself, and I believe him. It is a primal reaction, one where our autonomic nervous system (ANS) takes over. Once in control, the ANS is concerned only with survival. This innate desire to survive triggers a fight-or-flight response. When the ANS opts to fight, it fights to the death. On this date, it was almost death for at least one person. One of the victims suffered a brain injury after being struck in the skull by the metal weapon. His skull was fractured, and he suffered a subdural hematoma, bleeding within the brain. The man would suffer for the remainder of his life due to Nicky's blackout rage.

Nicky was forced to speak with a psychologist to evaluate his claims. In criminal law, almost every crime considers the element of intent. We call this *mens rea*, Latin for "guilty mind." Without a guilty mind, one cannot be guilty of an offense. To have the requisite guilty mind, one must be able to appreciate the wrongfulness of their conduct. The psychologist's report would determine his fate. Based upon my calculations, I had already been conceived at this point. My fate was tied to the results.

If Nicky were somehow absolved of responsibility, it would be time for the family to relocate. He was out of control, and the enemies he had made would be seeking their retribution. Rumors of vigilantism and comeuppance were spreading, and Grandpa Nick knew it was time to flee the city. An ill-thought-out business decision would force him to put these plans into action.

BANKRUPT BY BUSCH

The Sand Dunes Buggy Shop grew on the backs of Nick and Sam's relentless work. Word of mouth spread like wildfire, and racers from across the state were clamoring for a Sand Dunes buggy. Their frames, known for their resilience, could withstand the harshest terrains, and their meticulously crafted 1600cc Volkswagen engines delivered unmatched power. A buggy manufactured by Sand Dunes fetched a premium, and their reputation made them the go-to guys for rail buggies. They made sales faster than they could churn out product. With demand high and supply limited, they raised the prices of their premium machines. Even at those elevated prices, a waitlist formed, and professional racers begged for a spot, offering substantial sums to skip the line like anxious nightclub patrons.

One day, the shop received a call that would change everything. Sam answered in his customary fashion, "Sand Dunes." "Hello, sir. I'm an executive with Anheuser-Busch," a professional voice responded. "We'd like to set up a meeting with your management to discuss the purchase of some buggies." Sam, unconvinced, replied, "Come on in. We'll sell you as many buggies as you want to buy." As the back-and-forth continued, however, Sam's skepticism faded. He turned to Nick and whispered, "It's Anheuser-Busch. They want to buy some buggies."

A meeting was arranged between the suits from Anheuser-Busch (AB), Nick, and Sam. The AB representatives, led by a charismatic executive named Mr. Harrison, explained their needs. "Gentlemen," Harrison began, flashing a disarming smile, "Anheuser-Busch is launching a dune buggy racing series, a showcase of speed and skill in the most challenging off-road conditions." The series was to feature professional racers driving in different off-road environments, primarily desert settings. Each buggy had to be a premium machine, with blueprinted engines designed for maximum power and efficiency. The AB corporate sponsorship decal would adorn the roof of each buggy, and each frame would sport a distinct color. AB requested to rush twenty buggies into production, and promised to order another twenty immediately upon receipt.

"We're proposing a partnership," Harrison continued, his eyes gleaming with enthusiasm. "Sand Dunes Buggy Shop will be the exclusive manufacturer of every buggy in the series. We plan to film the races and broadcast them on television. Sand Dunes can expect to be paid very well." Previously, the buggy shop had done well—but this proposal would bring it to unprecedented levels of success. The initial deal would net them a windfall, and Sam and Nick would quickly become millionaires.

"Time is of the essence," Harrison emphasized. "We want to launch this series as soon as the first twenty buggies are complete. We'll also need Sand Dunes onsite for races, providing parts and mechanical assistance when mishaps occur. We'll compensate you handsomely for that as well, of course." A handshake sealed the deal, and pleasantries were exchanged before the AB executives departed. As Harrison turned to leave, he offered one final confirmation: "We need them done quickly, gentlemen. The cameras are waiting." The deal was sealed with a handshake. Nick believed that if a man shook your hand, he gave his word. That handshake should have been enough.

As was customary, Sand Dunes would purchase the parts and build the buggies as requested. Upon completion, a final inspection would take place, and if the buyer was satisfied, payment would be made. The Randazzo brothers needed to raise cash to purchase the parts—lots of cash.

Expecting repayment upon completion of the first batch, and for those proceeds to fund future orders, Sam and Nick each turned to their own individual property for collateral. By mortgaging their homes, Grandpa Nick and Uncle Sam barely raised the capital they needed. Some suppliers accepted invoices after delivery; anytime the brothers could delay payment, they did.

Having raised the necessary capital, they ordered the parts for the twenty buggies and began to work. Week after week, Sam and Nick slaved away, fueled by the hope of the impending payday. Unlike the sand rails they were used to building, these buggies were not for typical use; they needed special suspension and exhaust systems to handle the desert climate, and ran on high-octane fuel. Outside of AB's racing series, the buggies had little utility.

After working every waking hour between the agreement and the completion of the last buggy, they were finished. Sam and Nick celebrated, discussing how life-changing this project would be. But what began as exuberance would end in ruin.

Their work done, they called the AB executive as instructed. They left a message with his secretary, informing him that the buggies were ready for inspection. Days passed, and the executive failed to return their call. The brothers started to feel uneasy. Mortgage bills and parts invoices were coming due. During this exclusive project, they couldn't build any other buggies. Months without income had put them in dire straits. Then, they got the call.

"So, guys," the executive began, his voice lacking its previous warmth. "I was out of town. We discussed the project here at AB headquarters, and we've decided to place it on hold. We might revisit it in the future, but it's not in our immediate plans."

"That's fine," Nick responded, trying to keep his voice steady. "Just pay us for the first twenty units, and we'll hold off on the next order."

"I'm sorry, but that's not going to happen," the executive said nonchalantly. "We no longer need your buggies. You're free to sell them to your normal customers."

Sand Dunes Buggy Shop had met its demise because of a failure to get a written contract. Financially, Nick and Sam were ruined. The buggies they were left with had no value to their regular customers. Desperately, they tried calling their old clients, but the specialized nature of the AB buggies made them useless for recreational use. Without being paid pursuant to the terms of the contract, there was no profit to be had from the buggies. Their business was shuttered, and their homes were foreclosed upon. They had nothing left. With what little they could scrounge up, they headed for a simpler life. Grandpa Nick and Uncle Sam purchased a small piece of property outside of Arcadia, Missouri. Grandma Janelle and Grandpa Nick had just enough to buy a small camping trailer. It would be their home, and soon—with or without their son.

LABELED A BURDEN

After the St. Valentine's Day Massacre, the findings of the psychiatrist's report were revealed: "Dominick Randazzo Jr., at the time of the assault, lacked the capacity to appreciate the wrongfulness of his conduct." Nicky was going to be released. Barb rushed to meet up with her boyfriend; she had news herself. Not long into the film they were watching at the drive-in theater, Barb exclaimed, "I'm pregnant!"

I, most certainly, was not the plan. I know that my dad has always lived his life full throttle. I suspect that his alcohol and drug use was heavy during this period, and that this relationship was nothing more than a conquest for him. As for my mom, I suspect that her psyche had been compromised by years of severe trauma and substance abuse. I also suspect that neither of them slowed down until after my mother was deeply entrenched in her pregnancy. I wonder how their substance use impacted my development in utero. I wonder if the strength and depth of my mom's perseverance protected me from the substances that were being introduced, filtering out the bad and replacing it with pure love. This resilience is a trait she still possesses today. She continues to shelter me from the ills of the world, and frequently discomforts herself so that I will be left with a positive experience.

The drive-in's screen flickered with images of happy couples, a cruel contrast to the turmoil that churned within my mother. Outside the car, the respectful courtship between the lovable jock and a spirited cheerleader would lead to a fairytale romance. The couple would fall in love and have the baby that they both deeply desired. But that type of thing is only for the movies. I suspect that the revelation of my conception was not met with the normal joy a loving couple would experience after a lengthy period of trying to conceive. I suppose that the reaction was fear and panic. Why did they decide to keep the baby? After all, they could have a clean break if they'd just had the "procedure" done.

Maybe my mom ignored the signs that she was with child long enough to not have to decide. Maybe these two seventeen-year-olds had a mature conversation about becoming a family and raising a child. Maybe my mom just needed someone to love her unconditionally. This was a GOD moment. By all odds, my story should have ended there. Similar circumstances would undoubtedly lead many adolescents in the opposite decision. My story is only being told because of that choice, a choice that millions of other women have not taken. Why did I deserve a chance?

I was due at the end of September. Knowing that, Nicky divorced the wife he had taken when he was sixteen, and the expecting parents rushed to get married before they had the baby. My mother had to get a special wedding dress to accommodate her midsection, enlarged because of her pregnancy. They set their wedding date for August 25, 1984. That evening, Mom went into labor.

As the story goes, she traveled to hospital where she expected to see her obstetrician. Upon arrival, she was met with Doctor Armantrout. Doctor Armantrout was not her obstetrician. Hospital staff relayed to my parents that her usual doctor was on vacation for the next week, and that emergencies were to be referred to a coverage doctor. With no coverage doctor available, Doctor Armantrout was the next best option. His experience didn't involve delivering babies—at least, not human babies. Doctor Armantrout was a licensed veterinarian.

The consensus between professionals was that my mom was not far enough along in her pregnancy to deliver a healthy baby. Medication was given to her to delay my arrival. She was sent home and told to rest in bed, but even with rest, her body could only delay my arrival for so long. Multiple trips to the hospital resulted in the same course of action. On August 30, 1984, I was done waiting. Back to the hospital and the familiar face of Doctor Armantrout—but now, after nearly a week of labor, it was go time. Like he had so many times before with cows and mares, Doctor Armantrout assisted a mother in delivering a new life into the world.

Upon arrival, I was immediately rushed to the neonatal intensive care unit. My reward for finishing the race faster than most other babies was a weight of four pounds and some odd ounces and severely underdeveloped lungs. The course of treatment required for my maldeveloped body took us from Doctor Armantrout to a team of specialists. Actual medical doctors oversaw the first month of my life. I have been told that there was much speculation in those days about just how much life I might have. There were times when I was touch and go, times with some jaundice, and times when I was sick; the consensus was that I would never be a normal child.

The treating physicians prepared my parents for their future. My mom had now turned eighteen, but before my dad was old enough to vote, they received news that their week-old marriage would be burdened with a special-needs son. Specifically, I was going to be underweight and developmentally delayed. Communicating with me was going to require patience, learning would be tough, and they could expect their child to always struggle with social situations. I would always need special attention.

I can't help but reflect on that moment in time. If my parents could have hit the reset button on their decision to bring me to term, having known what they knew after my birth— would their answer have been the same?

Somehow, I survived these early difficulties, and was released to the world in September of 1984. The circumstances to which I was released were almost as meager as those within which I spent my first weeks. My first home was way out E Highway, on a gravel road that winds through the hills near Crane Lake, where my grandparents now owned a small piece of undeveloped land and a pop-up camping trailer. This type of trailer is basically a metal box that is opened by hand-crank, allowing tent material to unfurl out the sides. While it was adequate to shelter from the elements, it was no an alternative to four wood-framed walls and a roof. Noticeably absent from the pop-up trailer were indoor plumbing, running water, electricity, and a bed. The air inside was thick with the smell of mildew and desperation, the canvas walls offering little protection from the relentless Missouri heat. As an aside, I think this is where my aversion to camping comes from.

Inside this one hundred-square-foot dwelling, every earthly possession of Nicky, Barb, and Mike Randazzo was present. As if not packed enough, also residing in that space were my grandparents, Nick and Janelle Randazzo. Baths were taken at the closest water source, Marble Creek. The water was always icy cold, and I would shiver uncontrollably as my mom scrubbed the dirt from my skin. We lived off the land for a while. Those hills were abundant in wildlife. Habitual wildlife and game violations occurred, but we were fed. Those "crimes" were being committed, not to bag a trophy buck or a lunker fish, but to ease the hunger pangs of our dirt-poor family. Who wanted a trophy anyway? We had nowhere to hang it, and you can't eat the horns. That tradition of hunting has never been lost upon our family, a tradition that links us from a past of extreme struggles to a future that brought about different problems.

SHELTERED

That first winter of my life, it got cold. There was no heating mechanism in the pop-up trailer. We were miserable. I can still somehow recall the way the wind whipped through the gaps in the canvas walls, carrying with it the scent of pine needles and damp earth. The sound of rain drumming on the thin roof was deafening, and we huddled together, trying to stay warm and dry. Grandpa Nick finally decided it was time for a change.

The week of Christmas that year, Grandpa Nick returned to a career as an over-the-road trucker. A few days before the holiday, he left Poplar Bluff, Missouri with a load bound for California. Before he left, he handed over the last $5 that existed between the five of us, and gave the directive, "Get that kid something for his first Christmas."

Grandpa made the trip with no money of his own in his pocket: his gas was paid for, and he took with him only an oversized bag of sunflower seeds, a gallon jug of water (which was free to fill up at gas stations), and the determination to shelter me from the harshness of life. That trip altered the course of my life. From that point forward, Grandpa Nick would be the primary provider in my life. His sacrifices, and to a lesser extent, the sacrifices, Mom, Dad, and Grandma Janelle made, ensured that I would have a chance. Grandpa

Nick was never a man of few words, but his actions still spoke louder.

With Grandpa making a good living, Mom was able to stay home and focus her attention on my growth. My mom refused to accept that I would be unable to learn. She had tremendous maternal instincts for someone who was so young and so traumatized. I remember one time when I was sick with a fever and my mom stayed up all night, holding me in her arms and singing me lullabies. She wouldn't leave my side until I was feeling better. Some other members of our family gave me some secondhand children's books; my mom wore those books out, reading them to me repeatedly. Her desire for me to thrive despite my environment accelerated my growth. I expect that the same mechanism that sheltered me from a fatal experience in the womb also allowed my brain and body to form properly. Something divine formed order out of chaos in my early years. I see evidence of God in the early miracles that nourished my body and developed my brain. Before I was two years old, I had begun to outpace my peers in both bodily development and intelligence.

Dad did little to assist in my care. He tried to work a few different jobs. While he has never been officially diagnosed with it, I am certain that he has attention deficit and hyperactivity disorder. His ability to focus on an object or subject at hand is almost non-existent. I am sure that the disorder was largely responsible for his inability to maintain steady employment during my early years.

Grandpa's wages from driving a truck allowed Grandma Janelle to remain at the house as well, and she became my secondary caregiver. Grandma Janelle was a kind and gentle woman, always ready with a hug or a word of encouragement. She was a constant source of love and support for me, and I knew that I could always count on her.

Eventually, just before the cold became too much to bear, Grandpa's work allowed us to afford a real house. In reality, it was a duplex apartment, but we were able to rent both sides. Grandma and Grandpa lived on one side, and Mom and Dad lived on the other. We still spent time together every day, ate meals together, and did most everything as a unit.

Once Grandpa Nick had traveled many millions of miles in the cab of his International, he finally saved up enough money to begin our ascent from nothingness. Returning to the land where I made my first home and lived that minimalist existence, Grandpa Nick became the architect of our future. With money to purchase supplies, he began the construction of a home. He and his band of volunteers, comprised of any family member that would help, tirelessly worked to erect something we could be proud of. He spent his reserves to frame the house, and would have to return to truck driving many times to finish the project.

With the shell completed, Grandpa began to collect cardboard boxes. What other people discarded as waste, he used to insulate his home. Once enough material was collected to line the walls, excess cardboard was used to construct temporary rooms, and we began to stay in the house full-time. The floors were still bare plywood, with no covering but the cheap rug placed by the front-door opening. Learning to walk on this surface was challenging; frequently, splinters had to be removed from my hands, feet, and toes.

Grandpa continued working on the house little by little. Indoor plumbing was installed, then kitchen cabinets, and finally a woodstove to ensure that year-round living would be possible. Eventually, the final additions came along. I remember the celebration when the floors were finally carpeted and we were able to purchase our first pieces of furniture. It is amazing how little, yet how much we had at that time. We had everything that we really needed. We had each other.

The next few years were not too eventful. Mom continued to teach me. My mind and body continued to outpace the "normal" children of my age. I began to memorize random facts about dinosaurs from my books. My family was proud of my intelligence; Grandpa Nick and Mom were always quick to share the story of the "impressed entrepreneur." That story goes like this: just after I turned three years old, we were traveling to visit my "Country Family" (that is what we called Grandma Janelle's family who lived near Greenville, Missouri. I even called Grandma Janelle's dad "Country Grandpa"). We stopped at a store along the way, and I was introduced to the owner. Toy dinosaurs lined the shelves of the store. The man asked me if I liked dinosaurs, and I began to pick them up one by one and tell him their sizes and names. The man was impressed. He asked if I had any other tricks, and I responded by naming all of Santa's reindeer. After I listed Dasher, Dancer, Prancer, Vixen, Comet, Cupid, Donner, Blitzen, and Rudolph, the man was floored. He congratulated me by letting me have those coveted dinosaurs.

The child that was barely given a chance was thriving in this supportive environment. But soon, our family would grow, and the dynamics would change.

SIBLING RIVALRY

Most people search their whole lives for a best friend. I can picture the exact day I met mine. Grandpa Nick, Grandma Janelle, Grandma Sandy, Aunt Ronda, Aunt Lisa, and my three-year-old self huddled around the small viewing window, waiting for my mom and Dad to emerge with their prize. This is one of my first real memories—something even my toddler brain knew to enshrine in my hippocampus. Eventually, my dad entered the room with a tightly swaddled infant. As I laid my eyes on Kevin for the first time, I knew I was responsible for his wellbeing. Nothing was going to hurt my brother. On January 19, 1988, I became a protector.

My dad was an only child, and my mom had only her two older sisters, so I was unsure what it would mean to have a younger brother. The nearest example I could find was the relationship between Grandpa Nick and Uncle Sam, and the comparison was befitting. The similarities between how those brothers lived their lives and how Kevin and I have lived ours are mind-blowing. Approximately the same age difference existed between Uncle Sam and Grandpa Nick, with my uncle being the elder. Nick and Sam were born as brothers, but they chose to be best friends—Sam a little more reserved and more protective, Nick more of a gambler and less inhibited. Their relation was about reciprocity. Ours would be too.

Kevin was a fair-skinned, white-haired brute of a child. He inherited his blue eyes from Grandpa Nick, the unique tint of which made him stand out from his brothers and sisters. Sometimes, a glance into his eyes eases the absence of Grandpa Nick from my life.

Perhaps as a result of his lineage, Kevin also came to find hand-to-hand combat the easiest method to settle a dispute. During the pauses between screaming fits, I remember him launching rattles like grenades from his crib whenever he heard an unsuspecting visitor approach. I suspect he took some sort of pleasure when he struck his target.

From the time he started to walk, he would frequently challenge me to fight. His goal was to show that he was a formidable opponent for his older brother; my hope was to escape each of these encounters unharmed and with Kevin contained. Unknowingly, our scraps made us both better at our roles in life—him the fearless challenger and I the calculating protector.

The bouts between us increased in their potential for serious physical injury. Kevin ascribed to the Randazzo School of Fighting, the motto of which was "Win at All Costs." The speech that my grandfather had given my dad was soon given to us boys. Our dad, not known for his sage life advice, repeated the message that had been engrained in his own head: "Son, don't let people put their hands on you. If they run their mouth, you hit them first. You get the first lick in. There are no rules in fighting. The goal is to inflict more pain on them than they do on you. Never give up. If they are bigger than you, don't back down. Bite 'em, pinch 'em, poke their eyes. If that don't work, pick something up and hit them with it."

Kevin always gave me everything he had, but I viewed our bouts more as practice, sparring sessions. Kevin was a southpaw, and it only took a few left hooks for me to understand I had to control his left hand. Seldom did I lose my cool, entering each contest with a calculated approach.

By our teenage years, our fights had grown less frequent but more severe, and a few times they did get out of hand. One such fight occurred at home. Mom had found work outside of the house by this time, and we were often left home together. More times than not, we alleviated our boredom with fisticuffs. This particular scrap lasted almost an hour, including momentary breaks to catch our breath. By now, I had become adept at grappling Kevin so that he could hardly move. On this night, his determination overcame my ability to contain him. Bloody faces, a broken couch, a smashed vase, and a destroyed statue were the results. It was a close call, but the consequences were quickly cleaned up before Mom got home.

A more severe encounter happened about a year later at Grandpa Nick's Carlot, a second home for the two of us. I was sixteen and Kevin was thirteen. Around those ages, we were—for once—about the same size. Pulling up to the establishment, you would see large plate-glass windows encircling the office. Roller garage doors allowed access to the mechanical light, second bay, and paint booth. The office door was constructed of a metal frame and transparent glass panels. Upon entering the office, Grandpa's desk was situated on the opposite wall in the center of the large room. To the right of Grandpa was the entrance to the bathroom. The bathroom door was heavy, with an opaque window in the top portion.

On this day, as usual, the office was filled with family, each of us sitting and discussing the happenings in our lives. Grandpa sat at his desk, puffing away at a Winchester, smoke climbing to the ceiling and settling back down upon the room's occupants. He sat at his desk as if it were his throne, the Carlot his castle, and us his subjects.

Kevin was determined to aggravate me that day, more so than usual. The details are a bit fuzzy, but I remember him smacking me in the back of the head. He then laughed in my face—until he saw that I was angered. I rose from my chair and Kevin bolted, a move atypical of his character. I'm not sure what made me so mad, but I am sure that Kevin knew this was not an ordinary reaction. I gave chase. The closest barrier to hide behind was the bathroom door. Before I was able to apprehend him, Kevin had slammed the door shut. I attempted to overpower him and push it open, but Kevin quickly secured himself by latching the lock.

My rage built, and he began to shout insults from the other side. "You're too fat and slow to catch me!" "Come out and see what happens," I barked back. He did not oblige. What he did was worse: he placed his face against the glass. I could only see his silhouette, and I threw a punch with all my might, somehow punching clear through the glass and connecting with Kevin's head.

What began as shock turned to fear, as everyone in the room waited to see if Kevin would emerge whole. But for Kevin's extremely poor eyesight, he surely would have been blinded by the crumbling glass shards: his rimmed spectacles shielded his eyes, but pieces of glass had to be removed from his cheeks and forehead.

I felt miserable, shameful, and full of regret after the Carlot incident. How could someone who is supposed to be a protector inflict a nearly blinding blow to their protectee? I learned a lesson that day about underestimating my rage. I had only felt this remorse once before in my life and, similarly, it involved an incident that resulted in injury to my brother. We were both highly competitive, and almost always equally-matched, but there was one sport where Kevin was my inferior: he couldn't skate. I loved playing hockey, having grown up watching Brett Hull break records and having my heart broken by St. Louis Blues teams that could never quite win the Stanley Cup. While I only got to play one season of organized roller hockey, that didn't deter me from wearing out every bit of concrete I could find. I needed someone to play with and could seldom convince anyone to strap on the skates—but one time, I managed to convince Kevin.

Kevin elected for a set of adjustable quad skates, the type you would see at roller-skating rinks. I preferred the cutting-edge inline skates. Kevin was never comfortable having wheels beneath his feet, and I'm sure the combination of his pigeon-toes and weak ankles made for a painful experience. I rarely got a chance to show him up like this, and I took advantage of it. I stick-handled in and out of Kevin's feet, speeding around him many times as he did his best to remain upright. Finally, I tossed a loose puck a few feet ahead of him. He attempted to retrieve it, his skates clanking on the ground as he tried to step toward the rubber disk. I knew that was my chance: I lined him up, skated swiftly toward him, and delivered an explosive hip-check. Kevin fell directly to the ground and began to cry. I knew it must have been bad— Kevin never cried.

Mom gathered him up and asked what happened. He tried to mumble through his screams, but I interrupted, "I accidentally collided with him, and he fell." Lying to my mom was not easy; in fact, it added to the shame that I felt for injuring my best friend. Kevin thought it was cool that he got to wear a cast on his arm, but I would not soon forget how utterly I had failed at protecting my younger sibling.

We never let our fights affect our relationship. Like heavyweight fighters who embrace after a slobberknocker, once the fight was over, it was really finished. Instant amnesia would lead us back to harmony. Our goal was only to one-up the other, never to cause lasting harm.

A KEPT SECRET

With Kevin joining the family in early 1988, there were now six of us, and we were running out of room. Mom, Dad, Kevin, and I moved into an apartment in town. Grandpa Nick and Grandma Janelle continued to live in the new house. My grandparents, having had the consistent presence of a child in their home for the last few decades, knew that a change was coming. Grandma Janelle had had a hysterectomy sometime after Dad was born, leaving him her only biological child. But soon after Kevin arrived, an opportunity presented itself for Grandma Janelle to become a mother again—but it would require keeping a secret.

Grandpa Nick and Grandma Janelle always wanted more children. They learned of a mother who was pregnant and had decided she was not going to keep the baby. After some discussion, the forty-year-old couple resolved to keep their secret—a family pact that we were forced to abide by.

Grandma Janelle announced her "pregnancy" and then sequestered herself for the following months. Grandpa Nick, Dad, Mom, and Grandma made a pact that no one should know the baby was not their biological child. They figured I was too young to suspect any difference. While they were able to convince most other people of their story, I somehow knew better.

In the late 1980s, handheld cameras became more readily available to the public, and one of my Grandpa Nick's friends had splurged and purchased one. One afternoon, Ron Walton (a man who was in no way connected to Ron number 1 or Grandma Sandy's Ron) entered our house with a bulky bag in hand, inside of which was the device that would transform Ron into a director.

He methodically prepared to capture his shot. First, he needed to remove eight D batteries from their packaging, placing them one by one into position. Next, Ron removed the VHS tape from its wrapper. He pressed a button, and the side of the camcorder opened to receive the videocassette, just like the VCR would. After the lid was closed, he pressed the power button. A quick glance through the lens, and he was ready to shoot.

Even at that tender age, I did not shy from the camera. The director made it clear that I would be making my debut in his production, but what I didn't know was that I would have two costars. Before he hit record, Ron called for Kevin to be brought into the frame. He instructed me to play with my baby brother as he filmed. After a few seconds of playing, our shenanigans were disrupted by a knock on the door.

The director kept shooting. The door handle turned, and in walked Grandpa Nick, Grandma Janelle, and the new addition, bound tightly in a pink blanket. They walked toward my brother and I, who were still playing on the floor. For the camera, Ron proclaimed, "Well look who it is! Nick and Janelle coming home from the hospital with their baby girl. Let me see baby Dawny!"

She had been given a different name by her birth mother, one that I have never heard. She was introduced to the camera as Dawn Renee Randazzo. This manufactured production was meant to help cover up the secret. Unfortunately for everyone involved in the conspiracy, I went off-script. A young Mike asked, "Grandma, how did Dawn come from your belly? My brother came from my mom's belly, and she got fat. Did she come from your belly?" A long pause, and off camera Grandpa can be heard responding, "Yeah, she came from her belly, too."

I never fully committed to the charade. A natural-born child of my grandparents would be my aunt, and I refused to refer to Dawn by that title. While I didn't understand the fraud that was being perpetrated, I somehow knew that participating in it was wrong. I don't fault them for their attempt at deception, however. Answering questions about why and how are not easy. They wanted to raise Dawn as their real daughter, and their relationship could not have been more real if they shared genetics. (I regret not calling her Aunt Dawn. I would learn later in life that sharing blood is not a requirement for being family; sharing a bond is.) Kevin, Dawn, and I would be raised together, more like a sibling group than what legally it was.

SLICK SALESMAN

Throughout most of his adult life, whenever Grandpa Nick was not working on cars, he was seated in them, driving across the country as a truck driver. But after building his house, the allure of driving his big rig across the United States began to wane. Grandpa wanted to be home with his family, so he needed a new plan. He decided to pursue his passion for buying, fixing, and selling cars, and Rand Auto Sales was his solution.

Grandpa settled on the name after much contemplation. "Randazzo Auto Sales" had a nice ring to it, but he knew how often people butchered his last name. Throughout his life, he was called Dominick Rand or Nick Rand, with people often pausing to struggle with the rest. So, he settled on just that: Rand Auto Sales.

Originally, Rand Auto Sales employed Grandpa Nick and Dad. Eventually, everyone in our family would work there. Grandpa had a knack for looking at a product and intuitively knowing what he could sell it for. He could differentiate between cosmetic defects and structural damage, able to look past the dirt and wear. His mind could look past what a product was and discern what it could be. He was able to sell hope, the hope that changes your lot in life. The hope that tomorrow can be better than today. This skill would prove worthy in both the car business and in dealing with humans.

The Carlot was a lot of different things. Primarily, it was a business, even if you couldn't tell at times. It was a family hub, often a base of operations for whatever else was going on. It was a daycare. Sometimes we would gather there and eat whatever Grandpa Nick cooked up — on those days, it was a five-star restaurant. It was a therapist's office, a church, a pharmacy. More than anything else, it was a gathering place for lost souls, always attracting people who were down and out, defeated by life.

Starting with its very first sale, the Carlot turned a profit. Everything we had was invested in the business. With there being so many mouths to feed, there were times when the bank account balance would dip into the negative—but Grandpa Nick always found a way to make a deal and, in his words, "put us right back on the top shelf." There were also times when Grandpa had wads of cash to share with others, like a mother bird feeding her little ones. And that was the arrangement: all money would be funneled through Grandpa Nick.

The Carlot only took cash payments. A cash business, as Granpda Nick's dad had taught him, was near impossible to audit if the federal government started looking into your finances. Grandpa wouldn't take checks, and I watched many deals fall through because he insisted on the purchase being paid for in cash. The speed and accuracy with which he was able to count money was unrivaled. He would speed through a stack of bills like a card dealer at a casino, and his count was never light. You would never second-guess his total.

The basic pay structure for Carlot employees was a weekly salary—usually $100 for salesmen and car washers, $250 for mechanics, and $200 for painters. The base pay was always meager, and even my dad, who was a partner in the business, made less than minimum wage. However, commission often made up for the low base. The salesmen got $100 per vehicle sold, and the others got $50. Everyone was paid when we sold a car, as long as they were at work that day. If you missed work, you were docked the day's pay and any commission that you could have earned.

Grandpa offered a discount for paying in cash and in full at the time of purchase, and he offered in-house financing if customers didn't have the cash. There was an additional charge for this financing, but we never charged interest. Nick never ran a credit check when providing financing, and this allowed those who were turned away from other places to buy a car here.

The inventory consisted entirely of vehicles between five and fifteen years old. That was the sweet spot that Grandpa and Dad had identified to minimize their investment and maximize their profit—a formula that would allow the Carlot to grow exponentially.

Income tax season is the busiest time of the year for a dealership. Grandpa always described "money burning a hole in people's pockets" in late April. Where I'm from, the only time that most people had enough money to buy a vehicle was when they received their income tax refund check. We had to be prepared with something for them to buy with that burning money. The beginning of the year always began with a trip to the auction to purchase inventory and stock the lot. The Carlot always sold more vehicles between February and April than it did for the remainder of the year. From New Year's to May Day, it was all hands on deck.

Grandpa oversaw business at the Carlot much like how Uncle Mike ran his "family." Customers were expected to pay on time each week, and a failed payment meant collection efforts. Those efforts would start with a pleasant phone call. "Hello, Mrs. Johnson," Grandpa would say. "I see you missed your payment this week. You know I will have to charge late fees: $5 per day for every day you are late. If you are thirty days late, we'll have to come get your car." After two or three weeks of late fees, the next step in the collection effort would be a sterner phone call: "When are you going to pay me my money? You will pay me one way or another. If I have to repossess the car, I will make sure it costs you a lot more than you owe." Grandpa kept meticulous handwritten records, and when his records indicated that someone was a month behind, they were now the target of his anger. He would send one of his "repo men" to get the vehicle.

These repo men were typically large, tattooed, seedy-looking characters, the type that you would avoid eye contact with when passing on the street. They looked mean, and they were, when they needed to be. They were his henchmen— his hit men, if you will. Their job was to get the car back by any means necessary. Whether through direct questioning, deception, or destruction, these men needed to complete their mission before they were paid. The more "work" they needed to do to return the car, the more they received for their efforts.

The remainder of the staff was expected to make money for the Carlot and bring it directly back to Grandpa. He would decide how and when to distribute the proceeds of the business. Most of the time, they went directly into his pocket. The arrangement would turn out to be a bad deal for Dad. While he was supposed to be a fifty-fifty partner in Rand Auto Sales, Dad was allowed just enough to pay his own bills and keep Mom, Kevin, and I fed. Because of this arrangement, we were at Grandpa's mercy if we needed something. The Carlot always supplied my parents with a car to drive, but saving to buy anything else was tough.

Grandpa Nick gave Grandma Janelle and Mom an allowance for birthdays and Christmas. Otherwise, we didn't get anything more than was necessary to keep the lights on. With that arrangement in place, we settled into our life structured around the Carlot. My mom wasn't allowed to work, and Dad was only able to document earning $600 per month. Mom, Dad, Kevin, and I lived far below the poverty line. Mom sought welfare benefits, and the government provided us with insurance, a monthly check, and food stamps—three things we desperately needed.

With Grandpa hoarding all the money, the Carlot was making enough to start investing in classic cars and race cars. Grandpa knew how to construct an engine and oversaw each build. His specialty was classic Chevrolets. Many Chevelles, Camaros, and Corvettes made their way into the shop to be retrofitted with new powerhouses, engines that dwarfed the stock V8s placed in each by the factory. First, the mechanic would build the engine to Grandpa's specs. Next, they would install the engine in the car. Finally, the painter would provide the car with a loud, flashy color. These weren't the type of cars that Grandpa Nick was used to selling, and he would typically have to seek out the right match for these "specialty" cars. But when he found one, the profits always made the effort worthwhile.

To meet self-imposed deadlines, working hours were whatever Grandpa set. Grandpa, Dad, the mechanics, and the painters frequently worked late at night or into the morning. It took a special type of person to work at the Carlot. You had to be all right with little pay, no room for advancement, long hours, and stressful deadlines. That attracted a certain type of person—the type that wouldn't or couldn't work elsewhere. Felons, addicts, and other untouchables were all welcome at the Carlot.

A sort of symbiosis existed. Working in a cash business meant working under the table. Grandpa could get away with paying his workers less if they didn't have taxes taken out. In turn, his employees wouldn't have to claim that income, and they could qualify for government benefits. Frequently, Grandpa would barter with them over their food stamps, offering them half of their value in cash. This, in turn, allowed Grandpa to feed his workers for half price. Food was always Grandpa Nick's love language. Every day he cooked or ordered food for the guys, an unannounced benefit that likely helped keep some of his workers loyal.

Originally, Grandpa had one major rule for his workers: no drugs or alcohol at work. Many people professed their addictions when seeking out a job, and that rule was always part of the talk he gave them. But Grandpa didn't consider it his business what people did in their free time, and he knew that their addictions would continue. In a way, he contributed to them, much like the way he overlooked the delinquency of his own child.

The problem with hiring addicts is that they are unreliable. When they are high, they are easily motivated to work; when they are coming down, you can't get them out of bed. Grandpa needed his workers to get things done much more than he cared to enforce their sobriety, so he always overlooked the telltale signs of an addict on a binge. In the early 1990s, the Carlot was overrun with alcoholics and potheads. The 2000s saw heroin and methamphetamine become the preferred substances of the mechanics and painters. A final change in the 2010s saw his workers addicted to prescription opioids.

Such was the way of the Carlot for all its years. The staff worked hard and played hard. Their hard work padded Grandpa's pocket and kept a roof over our head. Their hard play got many of them arrested. Grandpa Nick and Dad would learn that befriending the workers, making them feel like Carlot family, ensured they could continue to exploit and profit from the cheap labor. Making the workers feel part of something was a useful tactic. The Carlot often saw workers leave, only to soon return and beg Grandpa for their jobs back—and he always obliged. Continuing to work at the Carlot led to continued feelings of inadequacy. Grandpa knew how to deal with the forgotten—his own childhood and early adulthood had been shaped by that same underworld.

The Carlot dynamic mirrored the relationships that Grandpa, Dad, and the rest of our family had with each other. We were a lot like those wayward Carlot employees, with Grandpa as the all-powerful asset controller, Dad the loyal servant, and the remainder his baby birds, always chirping for their fill. While I didn't know any different at the time, Grandpa Nick was calling all the shots. He was the puppet master. He was the architect. He was the provider. He was the conqueror. Unbeknownst to me, I could only be what he allowed me to be. While he was a savior in previous chapters of my life, his unspoken fear of losing his relevance in our lives compelled him to exploit that relationship. And even then, he was more than relevant to me. He was still my hero.

COACH DAD

My formal education began when I was four years old. In addition to the first few years of homeschooling I received from my mom, I attribute my lifelong thirst for knowledge to the Head Start program I attended in Pilot Knob, Missouri. Head Start was created for low-income families: part schooling program, part free daycare, and part opportunity to socialize students prior to public schooling. Mom bore complete responsibility for Kevin and me, since Dad refused to participate in any of the traditional functions associated with caring for his children, and I suspect she needed a break. Head Start eased the burden of the young mother of two.

After a year at Head Start, I began kindergarten at Arcadia Valley Elementary School, where I remained a pupil until the end of second grade. Before this, we got a chance to move out of the cramped apartment the four of us lived in and moved into our first real home. A low-income, first-time homebuyer program allowed my parents to somehow qualify for financing.

The move to Arcadia meant a lot to me. We had a large yard, wonderful neighbors, and the ability to finally get a dog. The large space also meant room to play, and for the first time in my life, I remember starting to bond with Dad. He had been an excellent athlete, and he now tried to teach me what made him excel. Dad taught me to play baseball, and the more I fell in love with the sport, the more I felt loved by Dad. At age five, he taught me to throw, hit, and all the other basics of the sport, a sport that gave me so much, a sport that I am still in love with today.

Dad was one of the coaches of the first team I ever played on. As a six-year-old, I was one of the youngest kids on the Arcadia Valley Clippers, and probably only made the team because he was a coach. Being a coach's kid was hard, but I thrived. Coach Dad was different than normal Dad. He was focused, he was motivating, and he taught the game as well as he had learned it. However, he treated me differently than the other kids.

I genuinely believe that everything he did, he did to make me a better player—but living with a coach means they never stop coaching. I never fully understood this phenomenon until I coached my own kids. Rides home from ballgames were always a trying time: the focus was always on what I had done wrong, not what I had done right. Criticism flowed more easily than praise from my coach. I don't blame him for it; when I started coaching my own children, I often caught myself heading down that familiar path. Remembering those rides home from my childhood gave me more perspective than most. With my own children, I regret not having said "Good job!" when it was deserved.

Inadvertently, Dad might have taught me a lesson about self-reflection by coaching me the way he did. You should always have the expectation that you will do well, you should critically evaluate your failures, and you shouldn't expect praise. No matter how well you do, people will criticize your performance.

The best memories of my childhood were on the ball field, but by the time I had turned thirteen, his life had become more chaotic, and he was no longer able to commit to coaching. For the six years he did coach me, I was proud—proud that he was my dad, and even more proud that he was my coach. We won a lot of baseball games—championships, even. But more significantly, we formed a sports-centered bond. I believe that baseball may have been the only language my dad and I shared.

THE FIRE

The fall of 1992 brought a huge change into our lives. I remember being awakened by the ring of a late-night telephone call. Dad answered, and then said, "Barb, we've got to go." Frantically, we were ushered to the car by my parents, and we quickly raced towards my grandparents' house. While en route, I recall Nicky hyperventilating a bit while proclaiming, "Dad's house is on fire. Uncle Sam called it in. They don't know where Dad is."

The discussion led me to draw the worst conclusion, a conclusion that I thought was confirmed upon our arrival. The home was fully engulfed, the flames glowing brightly against the backdrop of the night sky. The lights from the emergency responders swirled around, firefighters were hard at work, and paramedics in an ambulance appeared to be working on a patient.

We knew that Grandpa Janelle and Dawn were not present, as the two of them were visiting Grandma's family in Greenville. As we parked in his driveway, Uncle Sam brought us up to speed. "Your dad is in the ambulance—but he is all right. I knew he was home because he had just left my house. I watched him walk across the yard, and when I saw flames, I called 911 and then ran over to the house. When I got inside, he was asleep on the floor. Smoke filled the whole house. I grabbed ahold of him and dragged him outside. He was breathing, but he was choking really bad."

I remember being comforted by this assurance, but still overwhelmed by the scene. The house was completely destroyed—my first home, turned to ash.

With nowhere else to go, my grandparents became the new residents of our third bedroom. Buying this house had allowed just a little freedom from Grandpa Nick's control. Unlike the previous time we had lived with them, this time they were living with us. This was my parents' house, their rules, and their way of doing things. Grandpa Nick couldn't live that way for long.

A settlement from the insurance company came quickly for my grandparents, and with it, the prospects of finding a new home. While they searched, they lived in the back office area of the Carlot, which was equipped with a shower, a television, a refrigerator, and a couch. Inside the couch was a hide-a-bed, a fold-out contraption that tucked snugly inside the base of the couch when not in use. During the search, Grandpa and Dad continued to work together at the Carlot in what was as close to harmony as they could get. The closeness of the two led them to conceive a grand scheme to reunite in one location. First, they would need to secure land. Next, Grandpa would build his house. Then, we would build our house. Once complete, we would sell our current house and move into the new place. We would all live next to each other as neighbors.

Their plan went off without a hitch. Just outside of Bismarck, they found the perfect property with fields, woods, electricity, and a well. Soon, it would be what Grandpa and Dad expected to be their forever-homes. Grandpa's house was built first and completed late in 1992. Our house was finished in the fall of 1993. I remember we moved in near the time the World Series was being played. My first memory in the new house was Dad and I watching the Blue Jays beat the Phillies after the Joe Carter homerun.

With the new house came a new school district. While Kevin and Dawn would be starting fresh in Bismarck as new kindergarten students, I was the new kid—again. Having to leave behind my friends and baseball team made the move even more unsettling. Another decision had been made behind closed doors, Grandpa's hold on the reins remaining tight.

When a new inmate enters a correctional facility, the other inmates watch intently, the corrections officers take note of their presence, and the warden investigates their background. My first day at Bismarck, I underwent the same sizing-up. Who was this new kid? But soon, I was able to challenge them all, in both the classroom and on the ball field. The nerdy kids would worry they would be replaced academically, and the sporty kids would worry about their status on the playground. Meanwhile, I was just looking for a friend.

SPECIAL EDUCATION

School became my sanctuary. My mother instilled in me a thirst for knowledge, and I knew that education would be my salvation. Scholastic achievements weren't inherited; they were earned. Being judged on merit, rather than my last name, felt liberating.

As a newcomer to Bismarck Elementary, my past was a blank slate. Unaware of my family's history, the community was free to speculate. And speculate they did: the Randazzos, they decided, were mobsters. It was an easy leap to make. What else did people know about Italians besides pizza, pasta, and *The Godfather*? "Mafia Mike," I'd hear whispered in the hallways. I knew the truth, but I never confirmed their suspicions. My silence, I would later learn, was seen as an admission of guilt. The truth was far more complex.

It didn't take long for my fourth-grade teacher to notice that I wasn't on the same level educationally as my peers. Patti Pinkley had a reputation at Bismarck. Her height, less than five feet tall, made her only slightly less intimidating. She was loud. She was intense. She was my advocate.

"Where did you say you went to school before?" she asked after a few weeks of school. By the tone of her inquiry, I knew she was implying that I was different. Mrs. Pinkley had taken an interest in me, and in my experience, that wasn't a good thing. At her request, and at Mom's insistence, I was tested for the special education program.

Anticipation of the test built, and I recall thinking that maybe I was inferior to the other students. Maybe I was behind where I was supposed to be. Maybe those doctors were right in their original assessment, and no matter how hard Mom tried to teach me, maybe I just wasn't retaining what I should have been. I was scared to take the test, somehow knowing that it would separate me from my peers, and I feared that separation would lead to isolation. Isolation would be bad for the new kid.

The test was bizarre, unlike any I had ever taken. While I don't remember every portion, I remember several involved patterns. I was given a sequence of numbers and instructed to predict the next number in the set. I was asked to do mental math, adding or multiplying two-digit numbers together in my head. I was tested on my verbal abilities and memorization skills. After each portion, I recall feeling oblivious to how well I was doing. I didn't even understand what they were testing. I was scared to get the results.

After the test ended, I couldn't wait to complain to Mom about the torture she had subjected me to. I complained about the length of time that the testing took and the interrogation tactics the examiner put me through. Mom seemed unfazed by my uneasiness; in fact, she seemed hopeful.

The next day at school, I was called out of class. Mrs. Pinkley accompanied me to the threshold of her classroom, where Mrs. Gottman—the lady who had administered my test—was waiting with a stack of paperwork. She looked at me through her large glasses and said, "We have your results back. We would like you to join the program." "Join?" I thought. "I have a choice?" The smile on her face somewhat relieved my fears. "We want you to be in the Gifted

Program." She explained that Gifted was for students who were ahead of their peers, and that, each day, students in the program would be taken from their normal classroom and given one-on-one and small group instruction with a Gifted instructor like her to enhance their learning and expand their education beyond the boundaries of a normal classroom. I looked to Mrs. Pinkley for her assurance that this was a good thing. She smiled brightly and gave me a comforting nod.

Thank God for Patti Pinkley! In the brief time we had spent together, she had seen something that she believed was exceptional in me. While self-doubt has always lingered, her belief in me would change the trajectory of my education and, ultimately, my life.

Each chapter of my life has brought with it experiences, sacrifices, and lessons to be learned, but my ancestors' curse has never been too far behind. The amount of sacrifices that have been made for my benefit is remarkable. Somehow, my mother knew the reward for her sacrifices would not just be a normal child, but an exceptional offspring. She willed that reward into being. She hoped it into reality. The lesson was hope: hope that I would not be the burden that everyone expected me to be. Hope that somehow, I could be greater than the sum of my parts. Hope that I would break the laws of karma and become more than I deserved to be.

Now, as I look back on those early years, I am filled with a profound sense of gratitude. Despite the challenges and hardships, my family created a loving and supportive environment for me. They taught me the importance of resilience, perseverance, and hope, and they instilled in me the belief that I could overcome any obstacle, no matter how daunting.

ALWAYS AN OUTSIDER

The town that became my surname, Randazzo, is in Sicily, located at the base of Mount Etna. The name might possess a certain mystique to some, but to me, it was always a stigma—a label that I would try to shake throughout my life.

In the small town of Bismarck, your last name determined your status. You were either born a member of the in-crowd, or you were stuck outside looking in. Newcomers were rarely accepted by those who had deep roots in Bismarck. We were active participants in the community: Dad coached baseball, and Mom volunteered her time to the parent-teacher association and as a room mother at the school, where she was responsible for planning events for her children's classes. Kevin and I played on baseball and basketball teams. We were allowed these roles, but the Randazzos could never truly assimilate into the exclusive Bismarck in-crowd. No matter how well I did, or how hard I worked, it was never enough to be acknowledged by "them." The Bismarck originals wanted their town to remain exactly what it was. Growth would bring about a new crowd, a crowd that couldn't be controlled by their existing power structure. The Randazzos were part of that new crowd.

That's not to say that I didn't make friends or appreciate the chances I got at Bismarck. I am forever grateful for the way certain people there treated me, and I have grown to appreciate the others' rejection. Like the cowboy who gives thanks to the bull that bucked him off, I acknowledge how a failed attempt can instill the determination to be more prepared for future encounters. Bismarck would grant me many moments of clarity — points in time at which I resolved to rise above that small town. Outside of the margins of Bismarck's approval, I would succeed out of spite, often lifting myself up out of the dirt, dusting myself off, and flipping the bull the bird.

It is apropos that a train station served as the center of the community. The tracks that bisect the town are reminders of what it once was, of a forgotten time when Bismarck was a thriving community. The train station connects it to its history. Gone are the days when Union Pacific hired locals to work at meaningful jobs for good wages. No longer used to sell tickets and board passengers, its primary use is a meeting area for the city council. The trains now speed through the city, destined for more deserving locations.

As despondent as I may seem about the city of Bismarck, I have tried repeatedly to gain acceptance into that community. Even though it would have been easier, I never really moved away. In large part, my desire to make a difference in the community helped shape my life. After being certified as a lawyer, I offered my legal services to the city for free. Each time a position opened in the city—be it city attorney, city prosecuting attorney, or municipal judge—I humbly applied and offered to donate my time as a way to give back and bank some social capital with the people whose blessing I had consistently begged for. While abundantly qualified and personally vested in the outcomes, I was never given a chance to work in the city of Bismarck. I still wonder, sometimes, why I am so driven to seek their validation.

SPLIT PERSONALITY

Maybe my brain never quite bridged the gap between its analytical and primal sides. My premature birth might have had something to do with it. Maybe it's just written into my DNA; some people are born with that type of storm in their blood. Even Jesus lacked restraint when he flipped the tables at the temple after being angered by the Pharisees. When our anger is properly controlled, men like me can effectively deter unrighteous violence. Unbridled, we will wreck the best-laid plans. Society needs warriors to be warriors when it is time to be a warrior, and those same soldiers to be docile at all other times. It became apparent soon after I arrived at Bismarck that my lack of control would be a perpetual struggle.

It started early. One afternoon, during a kickball game in fourth grade, something snapped. Later, I'd learn that this was my brain's way of handling threats: adrenaline, noradrenaline—fight or flight. For most people, blood rushes to the muscles and survival takes over. For me, the blood never quite makes it back to my brain. I remember nothing about the fight itself. One moment it was recess, the next I was in the principal's office. Mrs. Pinkley described the scene: me standing over a boy curled in the dirt, hands gripping the fence, kicking over and over, until a voice finally broke through. "He didn't respond," she said. "He was just… gone."

The principal gave more detail: the kid had pegged me in the head with a kickball. I'd gone silent, then violent. Bloody nose, bruised ribs, a trip to the nurse. "Do you have anything to say for yourself?" he asked. But I didn't. I couldn't. There was just a blank where the memory should be, and a shame that felt heavier for being inexplicable. I was kicked out of school for a few days, which was fair. But this wasn't a one-off event—it was a pattern. My own brain, my worst enemy.

In the classroom, I excelled. The work wasn't difficult. My real challenge was staying in school to do it, because my temper kept getting me sent home. These episodes cost me more than just grades—they cost me a shot at valedictorian, salutatorian, and the chance to give a speech at graduation.

Bismarck dances were a big deal, especially with so few students—the high schoolers and junior high sometimes had to combine to fill the venue. My junior year, my little brother Kevin was in eighth grade, and he brought a date. We ran in separate circles at the dance, but drama found us anyway. Someone asked Kevin's date to dance, Kevin took exception, and soon he and my classmate were fighting. By the time I heard, teachers were already breaking it up. Kevin looked rattled, but he was fine. My fear morphed instantly into anger.

As my classmate strutted out of the gym, arm raised like a prizefighter, I snapped. The last thing I remember is running towards him. Later, I'd hear the story from witnesses: I hit him hard enough to knock both him and the teacher escorting him through the exit doors. I straddled him in the hallway, raining down punches, until staff finally dragged me off. Mrs. Milner, one of my favorite teachers, got caught in the chaos and took a punch herself.

Suddenly, I was confronted by her husband, the principal, Mr. Milner—a military man not known for leniency. "You hit my wife!" he bellowed. I had no defense. I'd never have hurt Mrs. Milner on purpose, but my intention didn't matter.

The punishment was swift: two weeks suspension from school. But the real penalty came from Mr. Milner himself. I was to get zeros on all missed assignments, and no makeup work or contact with teachers was allowed. Before this, I had the highest GPA in my class. Two weeks was all it took to throw that away.

Back at school, I tried to salvage what I could. I met with each teacher and did every assignment anyway. Mrs. Milner, gracious even after what happened, let me make up some work and gave me partial credit. "That's the hardest I've ever been hit," she said, but she forgave me. Her husband did not. He intended to exact his revenge. One of the duties of the principal was to plan the senior graduation ceremony, which involved approving the speakers and their speeches. He made it clear that I would not be giving a speech at graduation.

His plan was subtle and effective. Over the summer, school policy changed. GPA would now be weighted, giving extra credit to certain classes—not the advanced classes I would be taking as part of the Gifted program, but those less demanding ones he knew I wouldn't be enrolling in. Just like that, my shot at valedictorian or salutatorian vanished.

So, I plotted my own way in. Three students gave graduation speeches: the valedictorian, the salutatorian, and the class president. I'd never wanted a spotlight before, but now I was determined. I ran for class president, and after rallying my classmates I easily won the vote. Milner wasn't happy, but I kept my nose clean. Still, near graduation, he tried one last time to take me out.

The choir room was in the elementary wing, where hall passes weren't required. One day, I got up during class to use the restroom. Milner saw me and demanded a hall pass. "We don't use them in choir," I said. It didn't matter. He marched me to the office and gave me a choice: three days of after-school detention, or corporal punishment. I chose the paddle.

He made a show of it, wielding the wooden paddle like a tennis racket. The first swing barely registered; I laughed. The second was harder, and I laughed again, not out of bravado but relief—he'd lost. That was the last time he had power over me.

When graduation came, I stood on that stage and gave my speech. Not as valedictorian or salutatorian, but as the senior class president—the title Milner couldn't take away, no matter how hard he tried. This was something new to me. That which was earned by merit could easily be taken away, but that which was earned through the will of people was much harder to disturb. To my classmates, I was the voice of the oppressed—to deliver "their" speech, my charge.

A YOUNG MOTHER

For all intents and purposes, I became a father at seventeen. I'm not sure the exact day, month, or time, but like most of the men in my family before me, I was a teenage parent. When Amanda came into my life, Jacob was part of the package deal. I was a junior in high school, and she was getting ready to graduate. Amanda became pregnant with Jacob when she was fourteen and gave birth when she was still fifteen. Amanda and I had been classmates since elementary school—then we became friends and, ultimately, eternal sweethearts.

Amanda came from a well-known family in our area. Even though I had heard tales of the Fishers who terrorized the town, I knew they were good people. They had deep roots in Bismarck. Amanda's mom was born Jaqueline Emling, and her dad was Bob Fisher. By the time I met Amanda, her parents had already divorced. Her dad, deeply wounded by the split, lived in a little pink house on one side of town, and her mom lived on the farm that she had inherited from her own father, John Emling. The road from town out to his farm still bears his name today—an honor I admired, even though it reminded me that parts of Amanda's family were stalwarts of the Bismarck in-crowd. Bob and Jackie each had their own flaws—but despite those flaws, I couldn't have asked for better in-laws.

Amanda was the last of Jackie's five biological children, and undoubtedly the hardest to rear. The divorce of her parents left Amanda unsupervised during her teenage years, and she did what unsupervised teens do. She drank alcohol, got into fights, and began to spend time with a much older crowd. Those behaviors led to Amanda's first sexual encounter. Amanda was attracted to his rebellious, bad-boy demeanor; he had spent a portion of his own juvenile life incarcerated for felonious behavior. He was considered an adult by the state of Missouri, and she was fourteen. A failed birth-control regimen resulted in conception.

A lost child's inattentiveness led to Jacob's birth. I think back on this moment in Amanda's life, and what a burden it must have been on the undeveloped shoulders of a child! Amanda's handling of this situation spoke to her character. Her headstrong defiance of the norm led to her decision to keep the child—a decision that wasn't reached without pressure to consider the alternative.

She knew that her body was changing. At first, she blamed it on the birth control medication and her irregular menstrual cycle. During those first few months, it was easier for her to be dismissive, but after the first trimester passed, her original conclusion was less certain. She was confronted with the alarming reality: she was with child.

I'm not sure how a fourteen-year-old goes about taking a pregnancy test. Having never asked Amanda myself, I can only speculate about how it happened. First, you need to round up enough money to buy one. Do you ask your parents to fund your purchase? What if they demand to know what the money is for? Do you beg someone else to assist? Surely, they would ask questions too. Do you save up your lunch money? Once you somehow secure funding, how do you get to the store? You can't drive, so someone will need to take you. After you enter the store, where do you go? Do you risk the awkward encounter with an employee to ask where the pregnancy tests are located?

In my imagination, I walk through the grocery store aisles with her. Up and down she walks, scanning every shelf for the device that would reveal her fate. Finally, she notices it, the sole item on her shopping list. The top shelf is a struggle for her 5'2" frame. She needs to be inconspicuous. She scans the aisle left, then right, then left and right again. She rises to her tiptoes and fully extends her arms; her fingertips graze the top of the box. She attempts to catch it, but it falls onto the floor with a clatter. Time stands still. Another scan reveals there were no onlookers. It is now time to march to the register, package in hand. She discreetly places the box on the conveyer belt, and watches its slow advance toward the register. She recognizes the cashier, and hopes the cashier doesn't recognize her. Amanda keeps her eyes focused on the floor so as not to make eye contact. The first attempt to scan the barcode is unsuccessful, and a second attempt yields the same result. Her anxiety grows as the worker continues to struggle with the test. Amanda's mind races as she prays that an announcement over the loudspeaker and a price check aren't in her future. The third time is the charm. Amanda hands over the money she had saved up by forgoing her school lunch for the last few days, and she walks out, test in hand, determined to get her answer.

I suspect she would arrive back home and head directly to the bathroom. She would read the instructions for performing the test, and she would awkwardly position herself over the toilet, urinate on the stick, and wait for the result. That wait must have been agonizing. Watching intently, the blurred result would begin to come into focus. Two pink lines would confirm her suspicion.

Back to reality, she knew she had to break the news to her mother, her friends, and the contributor to her condition. They all talked through her options, each making their preference known. "You could go get it taken care of. I know a place in Illinois that charges $100. You just show up and leave without much hassle," announced an older, experienced friend. In fact, most of the older girls that Amanda had surrounded herself with had their own experience with "the decision," and each of her peers had opted to terminate their own pregnancies.

"I could help raise it," offered her mother. "I'll watch the baby while you finish school. It is going to be tough, but we will get through this."

The baby's father wasn't as supportive. "You are in your freshman year of high school. How are you going to take care of a baby? Are you seriously thinking about keeping it?" questioned the man. His opinion suggested his belief about whose responsibility it would be to raise the child.

Despite the crowd of people pushing her to erase the result of her youthful mistake, she somehow reached the opposite conclusion. I must pause a moment to appreciate the gravity of the situation. Amanda was from a good family, and she excelled as an athlete on the volleyball and basketball courts. My own daughter Gracie is now the same age that Amanda was when she got pregnant—Gracie even looks just like her mother did when she was 14—and I cannot fathom Gracie being forced to make that decision. Many opportunities would be taken away from Amanda, and her life would be upended. Amanda knew it. She knew she wasn't going to have the fantasy life she had envisioned. She knew she was taking the hard way.

Amanda had to disguise her growing belly at school. The fashion of the time, oversized sweatshirts, helped her hide her secret from her classmates, teachers, and coaches. But not long after her sophomore year began, she would face her biggest challenge: volleyball season was upon her. Volleyball was the primary focus of fall sports at Bismarck High School, and reminders of the success of the volleyball program hung throughout the gymnasium. Much of that success is attributable to the coaching of Paula Aubuchon. Coach Aubuchon had a no-nonsense personality, and she demanded greatness from her players.

Hiding her pregnancy from her coaches would be Amanda's greatest test, and ultimately, it was a test she knew she would fail. The first practice, Coach Aubuchon yelled at her sophomore setter for being lazy. "Fisher, pick it up. Don't let that ball hit the floor," the coach barked. Amanda pushed on with all she had, but the rigors of volleyball were an increasing struggle. Amanda faced the limits of her body the day that she was forced to dive.

The ball was short over the net, and she swiftly shuffled her feet to try to reach the spot. She wasn't going to get there. "Dive!" the gym echoed in unison with Coach Aubuchon. Recklessly, she sprang forward into a prone position. Her chest hit the ground, followed by her stomach. Concern quickly set in. A conversation took place after practice, and Amanda was forced to give up her first love to ensure the safety of her developing child.

Amanda delivered a healthy child on December 30, 1998. To her surprise, the baby's father was there. She interpreted his presence in the delivery room as an expression of his love for her. She thought it foreshadowed happiness for the new family—but after that day, Amanda and Jacob received nothing but disinterest from him. Ultimately, his failure led both of them to my arms and to my heart.

After giving birth at such an early age, Amanda became a pariah. She had been a social butterfly, but the popular girls that were her friends before the baby began to ignore her.

She looked for work, but she was determined to complete high school, and needed to find an employer willing to accommodate her academic schedule. The best job she could hope for was fast food. Working after school and each weekend became normal for the young mother. Her only extracurricular activity was caring for Jacob. She exemplified the selflessness shared by so many women in my life.

HORSEMEN

The success of the Carlot, combined with Grandpa Nick's frugality, led to some savings that needed investment. The Randazzo family has a long history with horse racing, mostly involving losses from betting on horses that didn't live up to expectations. A smaller, more intriguing part of that history involved owning and training thoroughbred racehorses.

There are a few ways to acquire a racehorse. One is an outright purchase, typically at sales where horses are auctioned off to the highest bidder. Another is breeding and racing your own foals. The final way, and the one we always used, is claiming a horse.

Claiming a horse is a risky venture. First, the horse must be entered in a "claiming race." In a claiming race, each horse competing can be purchased for a set amount. A would-be buyer goes to the racing office before the competition and indicates that they wish to claim a horse in the race. Once funds have been verified, the prospective owner puts in a claim on the horse. As soon as the race is over, the ownership of that horse switches from the original owner to the claiming owner. The original owner gets the money for the claiming price and any purse money they won during the race. You can't get too attached: every owner who enters their horse in such a race knows there's a chance they won't be returning with it. Owning a racehorse is always a short-term endeavor; claiming horses can be emotional.

Claiming horses involved a great deal of skill and an equal part of luck. To be a competent horse claimer, you needed access to a racing form, a program, or specialized internet sites that provide detailed information. These guides detail the horse's racing history, breeding, workouts, and a Beyer's rating (a system that rates how well the horse ran). Armed with this information, people decide whether to make a claim. Those who do it well investigate the trainer, the owner, and the horse itself, sometimes sneaking into barns to check out the horse or surreptitiously watching it work and run.

One day, Grandpa Nick's nephew, Frankie, tried to convince Dad and Grandpa to buy some racehorses. After deciding to invest our entire life savings at another late-night secret meeting, Dad and Grandpa went into business with Frankie to acquire and train horses.

Dad started buying printed daily racing forms, trying to find horses he believed were worth the claiming price. Once he identified one, he'd travel to the track, do his investigation, and decide whether to put in a claim. More often than not, we'd leave without a horse. However, one trip to New Orleans would significantly change our lives.

New Orleans was the home of Fair Grounds Race Course. There, a horse named Table the Motion was inexplicably running in a claiming race far below her actual value. Table the Motion was a three-year-old filly who had already won five races and was on track to become a stakes horse—a horse that would run against the best in the country for high purses and couldn't be claimed. The speculation was that she was injured or had some other undisclosed problem.

After arriving at Fair Grounds, Dad and Frankie began their investigation. They found the barn where Table the Motion was stabled. Late that night, after everyone had left, Dad and Frankie sneaked into the barn and located their target. Approaching her stall, they observed a wide-backed horse with a line down the middle of her face that almost connected her forehead to her upper lip. The line was broken up between her ears by a white shape—a cross.

Frankie tried to enter the stall, but each time he did, she reared up, kicked, bit, and chased him out. She had spirit. Eventually, Dad held her head, allowing Frankie to pick up and inspect each of her ankles. He found no heat, bulges, or imperfections that would cause concern.

The next day, they watched the horse leave her barn and walk up to the track for her race. In the paddock, she continued her antics. As her trainer tried to saddle her, she kicked at him. When he placed the bridle over her head, she refused to accept the bit in her mouth. She was defiant. But after some discussion, Dad and Frankie decided to claim the audacious filly.

To officially claim a horse, you need sufficient funds in your horseman's account and must fill out the official claim paperwork at the racing office before the race begins. Racing officials confirm you have the funds and determine the process if multiple claims are placed on the same horse.

That day at Fair Grounds, Frankie raced into the office, where a large crowd had gathered. As he completed the paperwork, he could hear other trainers talking to their owners. Everyone was there to claim the same horse. Table the Motion was going to have a new owner after this race. After barely getting the paperwork complete, Frankie and Dad listened as the office worker announced, "Ladies and gentlemen, we have a seventeen-way claim on Table the Motion in this race."

Most of the time, claims are decided by a roll of the dice, known as "shaking for the claim." Whoever rolled the highest number won. But with seventeen claimants, a new system was needed. The racing director quickly decided that the prospective owners would draw popsicle sticks numbered from one to seventeen. Whoever drew the highest number would get the claim.

Anxiety and anticipation filled the room as the popsicle sticks were distributed. Dad watched as the other owners glanced at their numbers and then looked away in disgust. As the last to put in the claim, they were the last to get a stick. Frankie grabbed the stick and covered it entirely with his hand. He turned so that only Dad and he could see the number. Slowly, Frankie peeled his finger away from the first digit—a one. As he pulled his finger away from the second, the crooked top revealed their fate. Fully exposed for everyone to see, the number seventeen appeared on the popsicle stick in Frankie's hand. Table the Motion was our horse.

Soon, the filly affectionately known as Motion would become the talk of Fairmount Park (our home track in Collinsville, Illinois, about 15 minutes east of St. Louis). The Randazzo family was well known on both the frontside (where the betting took place) and the backside (where the barns were located). An infamous story about Frankie's dad was often told at the racetrack.

Frank Randazzo, Frankie's dad and Grandpa Nick's brother, was a massive man. Few people would dare to physically challenge him. A braggart, Uncle Frank often claimed he could throw a punch that could knock out a full-grown horse. He'd often solicit bets from those who doubted his strength. One fateful night, he was called to task.

A group of onlookers surrounded Uncle Frank as he rolled up his sleeves. An unsuspecting horse was led to the area. "One grand says you can't even hurt that horse," his bettor mocked as the animal was secured.

What followed was both impressive and repulsive (undoubtedly an act of abuse). Uncle Frank swung an overhand right, catching the horse on the left side of its face. The horse's eyes rolled back and it collapsed to the ground, motionless. Frank raised his arms in conquest. In disbelief, the man counted out ten $100 bills, and the infamous story began to spread.

Fairmount Park was Frankie's home track, and Motion was stabled in the Randazzo barn. Frankie had been a trainer for a long time, but he had never trained a horse of this caliber. Thoroughbreds are hyper by nature, but mostly docile and eager to please. Muscular, hardworking, and fast, these animals are superior in performance but often lack intelligence. Motion had both virtues.

The first night she stayed at the Randazzo barn, she was left in a tidy stall with a full bucket of grain and some hay. The barn doors closed, the lights went out, and the humans retired for the night. Frankie was the first to arrive early the next morning. As he slid the large end door to the side, he saw a shadowy figure at the other end of the barn. Walking in, he flipped the switch to illuminate the stable. It was in complete disarray. The shedrow, the walkway that centered the stalls, was not how he had left it the night before. The last task each night was to rake the shedrow so everyone could start the day with a clean surface. The webbing that normally blocked the entrance to one of the stalls was torn, its steel snaps shattered nearby. The stall had been destroyed, with holes dug in each corner and water and feed buckets dumped upside down. As he stepped over the empty feed bags and litter strewn about in the walkway, Frankie saw Motion staring at him, as if to communicate a message: "You cannot contain my spirit." And we never did.

While we'd end up owning many thoroughbred racehorses, Table the Motion was our honeypot. The first year we owned her, she ran through every group of three-year-old fillies, besting every challenger in her first three races for us. A filly is a female horse younger than four years old, while a mare is four years or older. The distinction is important, comparable to the difference between a teenager and an adult. Mares are more developed and experienced than fillies. Nevertheless, after easily beating all the fillies her age, Motion started running stakes races against the best mares in the region.

The reigning mare of the year at Fairmount Park was a horse named Appleshiner. She was the class of the track, having held the title for the previous two years, and drew crowds whenever she raced. After winning her first three races impressively, Motion was starting to gain recognition too. Seeking to capitalize on Appleshiner's popularity, Frankie decided to enter Table the Motion in a race against the mares. The head-to-head matchup was set for a Saturday night in June.

The talk of regional horse racing centered around the upcoming contest. As anticipation built, our confidence in our horse grew. Most horsemen voiced criticism, deeming it unwise to run the filly against the dominant mare. An easier race could be had against other three-year-olds with the same purse money. Why would the Randazzo barn risk their future against the best horse at the track? Undeterred, we were convinced Motion could slay the giant. So convinced, in fact, that a side bet of $5,000 was made between the owners.

That Saturday night was the greatest racing day I can remember. The track was packed shoulder to shoulder. Motion, nervous by nature, swayed her head back and forth as she walked to the track to be saddled, bobbing and weaving like a dancer. It was as if Motion could sense the importance of the race, and was locking in like any professional athlete. Our family, clad in Table the Motion hats and shirts, found our way to the finish line. Motion appeared to be walking on air as she pranced out of the paddock and onto the track. Cheers erupted from the crowd as she was announced for the race.

The horses entered the starting gate one by one. The final gate shut, and the world stood still. The crowd became almost mute. The long pause was interrupted by the bell. The track announcer started his call: "And they're off! Breaking clean are Table the Motion and Appleshiner. Table the Motion sucks into the rail as Appleshiner trails by a half-length on the outside. They continue around the first turn, and Table the Motion expands her lead to about one length over Appleshiner. The group continues down the backside as Table the Motion opens up a two-length lead. As they turn for home, Table the Motion has opened up a three-length lead over the rest of the pack!" The crowd roared as the horses raced down the track in front of the grandstands.

The announcer confirmed the result: "Appleshiner attempting to gain ground on Table the Motion, but can't! Winning handily, it's Table the Motion!" Jubilation ensued. I remember being high-fived by random people as they joined our celebration, and we raced toward the winner's circle. When your horse wins, a picture is taken in the winner's circle to commemorate the victory. That picture would be the second-greatest highlight of our horseracing careers.

Becoming queen of the track in Collinsville, Illinois is much easier than making a name on the national horse racing scene.

Racing at the national level is huge industry, dominated mostly by wealthy owners. In an attempt to become relevant nationally, we took Motion to the most famous racetrack in the business. About four hours east of Fairmount Park is the Mecca of thoroughbred horseracing: Churchill Downs in Louisville, Kentucky, home of the Kentucky Derby. Motion would run a race the day before the Derby at the same track.

Being the new kids is always a challenge. When you travel to a new track, it's called "shipping in," and you're placed in a special barn called the shipping barn. The shipping barn at Churchill Downs appeared to be one of the original barns at the track—run-down and lacking the amenities of the regular training barns.

While the backside of Churchill Downs was unimpressive, the frontside was filled with pomp and circumstance. It was surreal. I read the names of the Kentucky Derby winners in order, all listed on an enormous plaque above the paddock. Staring at the very same paddock that once corralled Secretariat, Citation, and Seattle Slew, I came to a name I recognized: Affirmed, the 1978 Kentucky Derby Champion. Affirmed would later become the grandsire of our very own Table the Motion. Standing there in the shadow of her grandfather at the racetrack that made him famous, Motion and I had something in common: we were on a quest to escape the shadows of our grandparents, determined to carve our own paths.

That day at Churchill Downs, Motion ran against a horse named American Dynasty. As great as Table the Motion had been, she couldn't outrun American Dynasty. In fact, in three attempts, she never did. American Dynasty would win the Oaks race that day and go on to win the National Filly of the Year award. Table the Motion finished fifth in that race and fifth in voting for National Filly of the Year.

Table the Motion would be the greatest horse we ever owned. The purse money she won funded our entire racing operation. Hoping to catch lightning in a bottle again, we used most of that money to claim new horses. While we had other horses that ran well, we never had another like Motion.

Being a teenager during that time was enjoyable. I experienced the fun side of horseracing, making money cleaning stalls, walking horses, and grooming them. We traveled from track to track, ate at nice restaurants, and saw the local attractions. Grandpa even neglected the Carlot operations so he could join in the fun. We were living the high life, as if it would last forever. But soon enough, the horseracing operation would disintegrate.

BEHIND THE GRANDSTAND
A World of Lost Souls

Behind every horse racetrack lies a hidden world, an asylum for the lost and neglected. Gambling is the most innocent vice you'll find there. A whole catalog of sins permeates the world behind the stable gates, infecting the horsemen who can't resist the lure.

Life as a horseman is grueling. Days begin before sunrise, preparing the horses for training. Each one must be led from its stall, walked, trained, and fed. Weekends bring no respite, with constant feeding and watering. Race nights often stretch past midnight, only to begin again before dawn. Horses sometimes have to be euthanized right there on the racetrack because of broken legs. It's a relentless cycle, running seven days a week, often 365 days a year. And neither the weather nor the horses always cooperate. This monotony only exacerbates the horsemen's vices.

In my experience, everyone drawn to the racetrack's backside is running from something. Addictions flourish there, cheaters cheat, liars lie, and exploiters exploit. The subculture is a self-contained world with its own government, police, laws, and economy. The locked gates, allowing passage only to licensed horsemen, create a perfect breeding ground for misbehavior. In effect, crime becomes normalized, almost legal.

Drugs are readily available, fueling the risk-taking personalities that gravitate to the track. Many undocumented immigrants find their way onto the backside, along with the homeless, drawn by the ridiculously cheap dorm rooms. These rooms offer little more than shelter and privacy to indulge whatever demons their occupants harbor.

The backside operates on a strict hierarchy. At the bottom are the grooms, who walk and clean the horses, working exceptionally long hours for less than minimum wage. When a horse wins, the groom might receive a small bonus from the owner, enough to ensure continued obedience, but never enough to escape their financial straits. Often, it's just enough to fuel their next fix.

Next up are the trainers. Some are blue-collar farmers who don't live at the track, salt-of-the-earth types less likely to get mixed up in the underbelly. Others are little more than grooms who've been around long enough to be promoted. These trainers are there for a quick buck, caring little for the animals' well-being. They're paid daily for training, with bonuses for wins. Their responsibilities include ensuring the horses are fit, vet-checked, and ready to race.

At the top are the owners, a far more homogenous group, almost always elderly, rich, white men. They call the shots and control the money. Grooms and trainers vie for the "good" owners, those who pay fair wages. Ultimately, this group benefits the most from the exploitation of vulnerable souls on the backside.

For a few short years, horseracing significantly improved my life. But, in our case and everyone's I knew who lived that lifestyle, it would take away far more than it gave. I don't know if it's the people who are attracted to this underground economy, or if the economy creates these types, but the racetrack slowly leeches away one's soul. Mirroring the gambling culture it supports, track people rarely know when to cut their losses and walk away.

That was our experience. When our mare was winning, money flowed freely. Accustomed to this steady cash flow, we believed our success would last forever. But as Motion slowed, so did the growth of the purses. We foolishly spent Motion's winnings as quickly as they came, supporting a newfound lavish lifestyle. It was unsustainable, unreliable, and just plain dumb business.

Dumb business led to dumb legal decisions. As mentioned, the racetrack attracts unwanted and undocumented members of society. Criminal elements see it as a unique opportunity to launder dirty money, turning illicit gains into documented income. Organized crime, following in the footsteps of the Sicilian Mafia, has found horseracing particularly attractive, and Mexican cartels have immersed themselves in the scene.

A FAMILIAR OCCUPATION

Around the time the cartels sank their claws into horse racing, our own racing operation began to crumble. We owned too many horses, and the expenses devoured any winnings. Regardless of how much they were losing us, all those horses still needed care. An opportunity soon emerged to keep the operation afloat: supplementing horseracing with selling narcotics and laundering money.

It started innocently enough. Christina came to live with us when she was about fifteen. She wasn't a blood relative, but calling her our cousin was easier than explaining the situation—she was the daughter of a friend of my mom, Donietta, and the stepdaughter of my dad's best friend, a biker. Shortly before she moved in, Dad's friend had seemingly overdosed—although rumors circled that he had been intentionally done in by a rival biker. He left behind a wife, two kids, and three stepchildren. With five young mouths to feed and unable to control Christina, Donietta asked my parents for help. Could Christina live with us?

After some discussion, Christina moved in. She would go on to become friends with Amanda; in some strange way, her living with us formed the connections that led to my relationship with Amanda. But, as is often the case in my life, this relationship also brought its share of unhappiness. Christina was a grifter, and after moving in she started dating

Jorge Trevino. He wasn't too much older than me, and we hit it off; Jorge was likeable, funny, and always treated me well. I enjoyed being around him, but I knew there was more to him. He inexplicably had a lot of money and nice things. In the early 2000s, large SUVs with oversized wheels were popular, and Jorge had several. I'd never even seen a Rolex in real life before I met Jorge—he had one for every day of the week. He wasn't too much older than me, and we hit it off pretty well.

Meanwhile, my dad was becoming more distant. I only ever saw him when he dropped off money for Grandpa. I grew suspicious of his activities. His stories didn't add up. Our horses weren't winning, yet Dad was bringing home "winnings." You can't win when you aren't winning. And I knew Dad was spending all his time with Jorge.

I was young, but not naive. My seventeen-year-old self suspected that Jorge was selling narcotics. These suspicions were confirmed one night when I asked to ride with my dad to a meeting with Jorge and his brother. I didn't see my dad often, so I was excited to go. During the trip, I overheard the adults talking about getting cash from a house and claiming a racehorse. By then, I'd checked out of horseracing, too busy playing baseball, partying, and chasing girls to waste my weekends at the track. Dad and Jorge were apparently becoming partners in the horse business—but I knew there was more to it.

Eventually, my wariness of Dad's business dealings was confirmed. The reality crept in: my dad was a drug dealer. What I didn't know was that he had developed deep connections to the Garcia-Serna Cartel. Jorge and his crew were running narcotics from Mexico to St. Louis. Decades ago, Grandpa Joe had somehow broken free from his own ties to organized crime; now, his grandson had returned to those roots. History had repeated itself: a member of the

Randazzo family had again run afoul of the law, and, again, his indiscretions would lead to family-wide suffering.

But how did they do it? Lots of drugs brought lots of money; lots of money brought lots of attention. The partners knew law enforcement was always watching, following, and listening. I remember Jorge and Dad were always buying burner phones, the cheap kind found at grocery stores. They were purchased with cash, activated, used up, and then destroyed so the line couldn't be tapped or traced. But how did the actual drug shipments evade detection?

Horse racing requires a lot of travel. To travel with horses, you need a heavy-duty truck and a horse trailer. The horse trailers are designed to keep the horses standing for the duration of travel, and they often relieve themselves on the floor of the trailer. To combat that waste, many horsemen put pine shavings or sawdust on the floor. It provides the added benefit of softening the ground the horses are standing on. When piled deep enough, those pine shaving could conceal large objects—packages of narcotics, for example.

Hauling horses from track to track across North America provided the perfect cover. Additionally, that pine scent masked the odor of the drugs, confusing police dogs during the many searches the trailers were put through.

Dad is a convincing person. He inherited his own father's ability to close a deal, and perfected it at the car lot. Grandpa Nick used to say, "If you can sell used cars, you can sell anything. A used car is usually one person's problem. You must see through the dirt and the imperfections. You have to see what the car can be, not what it is. You're selling the potential." In a way, he meant you were selling hope—that affordable car brings the promise of a better life. But Dad was selling his customers despair, heartache, and addiction.

He was dealing death, and soon, the relationships around him would die as well.

The age-old adage is that a drug dealer can't be their own best customer, and it makes sense: if you use your own product, you cut into your profit. I suspect Dad didn't start an addict—but when cocaine is readily available and the people around you encourage its use, the compulsion to use often outweighs the desire to abstain. Nicky became a user: first cocaine, then methamphetamine, and finally opiates. He remains haunted by his opiate addiction.

ABANDONMENT ISSUES

Grandpa Nick knew the writing was on the wall. By the time I was sixteen, he'd refocused on the Carlot. Dad, however, wasn't ready to give up the fast life, and stayed at the racetrack. And when I say stayed, I mean he literally didn't come home. I rarely saw him during this period; he was too busy hustling to return to the mundane realities of rural existence. He was focused on big cities, big people, and big times. By the time I was eighteen, Dad was just a visitor in my life. In some twisted way, he thought he was shielding Kevin and me from his illicit activities. But his absence had a profound impact: Mom was essentially a single parent. The two were de facto separated at this point—he wouldn't even pick up her calls. Mom was naive, but not dumb. She recognized what was happening. To salvage her marriage, she began to discreetly follow Dad, and discovered his addiction—and his infidelity.

I've never tried to justify his actions, but I've always longed to understand them. Was Mom not enough for him? Were Kevin and I so insufficient that he forgot about us, unsupported and suffering at home? Mom was forced to return to the workforce to keep the family afloat. Abandoned by Dad, she had to make ends meet for me and Kevin.

Ironically, she got a job at Fairmount Park. As a bookkeeper at the racetrack where Dad lived, she was bound to cross paths with him—I suspect this was her main motivation for taking the job. It was the only way for her to stay relevant in his life. Distracted by these duties, as well as a hurt heart and a desire to not be forgotten by the man she had devoted her life to, she also absented herself from significant portions of mine and Kevin's lives. Thankfully, we lived next door to Grandpa Nick and Grandma Janelle. Amidst the dysfunction between our parents, they were the only real source of emotional and financial support we had.

Being largely unsupervised seventeen- and fourteen-year-old boys wasn't all bad. I had a lot of friends in Bismarck. I wasn't accepted by the "right" people, but I became popular, especially with the high school and young adult crowd. The controlling families of Bismarck were not impressed by the crowds that had started to gather at our home on the weekends. Our opponents feared my family at this point. The Randazzos weren't puppets—we refused to assimilate into their ways, their hypocrisy that excused six days straight of sin as long as they were atoned for on Sunday.

During my junior year, another Randazzo boy came to live with us. Adam Randazzo and I shared a great-grandfather, Grandpa Joe, although neither of us ever met him. Adam's grandfather was Joe Jr., Grandpa Nick's brother. Uncle Joe had always owned racehorses, and Adam's dad worked at the track most of his life. We were the same age, and we often played sports or video games to kill time during the races. Soon, we were like brothers, and we devised a plan to live together.

Adam wasn't in a great situation at home. He played baseball and football at Jennings High, but he was an outcast. I saw him subjected to racism because he was the only white kid in his neighborhood. Honestly, I first encountered racism when Adam and I visited his mother. The AC in Adam's car didn't work, and we were sweating when we pulled off the highway into Jennings. As we stopped at an intersection, a group of African American men began to verbally assault us. "Get the fuck out of here, honkey! Fucking cracker! Better get your ass off this block, Casper!" they yelled. We managed to speed away before they could get their hands on us.

Adam was unsafe in that neighborhood. There was room at our house, and he could fit in on the baseball team. Once we'd ironed out the details of our plan, we approached our mothers. Unexpectedly, both approved. Now there were three boys living at the Randazzo home.

Adam and I finished our junior year of high school together. The following year, Adam and I were seniors, and Kevin joined us in high school as a freshman. We had one year left to make a mark, so the three of us stayed focused on school. During the week, we attended practice and did homework. On weekends, we looked for a place to party. Our house was the default if no one else volunteered theirs. For the most part, our parties were peaceful. We invited our friends and welcomed whoever else they brought.

Unwittingly, the mob mentality had permeated our social circle. We protected each other. When conflicts arose with those outside of our group, we united against them; if it came to blows, each of us was expected to fight. Most of my friends were older, which made it easy to get alcohol as a minor. Alcohol and absent parents made it easy to throw parties. We often held ragers in our basement—but while underage drinking was widespread, open drug use wasn't. In fact, I specifically made it a rule: no drug use at a Randazzo party. I'm not dumb enough to think that nothing went on, but those caught by me were banished. I'd taken a hard line: my friends didn't even talk about drugs around me. It might seem like a bizarre distinction—encouraging blackout drinking but forbidding anything else—but I'd seen the dangers of drug use, and viewed alcohol as less risky.

While parties were a fun way to kill time, I longed for something more meaningful: I wanted a girlfriend. I'd dated a few girls on and off, and I had been in one relationship that I thought was special—but it ended not long after Adam moved in with us. I guess I inherited my mother's naivety: I was being cheated on. The secret wasn't well-kept: embarrassingly, most of my peers knew that this girlfriend was unfaithful. Heartbroken, I was unsure how to move on.

Adam had established himself amongst my friends at this point, and began dating Kristie, the girl who would become his wife. Kristie and Amanda had been friends for most of their lives. Kristie was one of the few who didn't publicly criticize Amanda when she became a mother, and they grew closer during my junior and their senior years of high school. Eventually, they started hanging out almost every weekend. One weekend, Kristie wanted to go to the Randazzo home to see Adam and convinced Amanda to come along. At our house, Kristie and Adam were occupied with each other, leaving Amanda and me to entertain ourselves. I remember having the deepest, most engaging conversation of my life. We were both going through heartbreak and dealing with our parents' separations. Amanda's parents had officially split years before, but mine were still going through their de facto divorce. It's cliché to say it was love at first sight—I was already friendly with Amanda—but neither of us had seen the other as a potential partner until that day.

That night, in the basement of our broken home, the fractured pieces of her being somehow completed the puzzle of mine. Our talks turned into a romance, and our romance into exclusivity. The details were messy: she had a toddler and adult obligations, I had a promising future and no responsibility. But despite all that, over twenty-three years later, a relationship that seemed destined to fail has produced the greatest memories of my life. Every day I wake up and thank God for letting me return to this dream.

STAYING BETWEEN THE LINES

Baseball taught me almost every lesson I'd need in life. In fact, for a project in one of my children's language arts class, I wrote a letter to myself detailing those lessons. I've included that letter in its entirety.

A Chat with My Youth
by Judge Michael Randazzo

Dear eighteen-year-old Mike Randazzo,

It's your last year of high school. I'm writing to you from eighteen years in the future to offer some advice. Enjoy this year: it'll be one of the best of your life. Cherish every minute. You'll miss this. Never again will the balance of responsibility and fun be so heavily weighted toward enjoyment.

Though you realize it subconsciously now, you can learn everything you need to know about life on the baseball field.

Honor the game by playing it hard. Life is easy now, but it gets harder. Always be committed. Run out every ball. Play every pitch like it's your last, because one day it will be. Sometimes, you'll face impossible odds. Play anyway. You'll lose, strike out, and fail. Make failure temporary. Remember, a good hitter has a .300 batting average, meaning they fail seven out of ten times. Measure progress not by failures, but by successes. Trust the process; we learn more on the journey than from the result itself.

Enjoy the little things, whether they are a bloop single or just being on the field with your buddies. Life is short, and none of us get out alive. Make fun of yourself. Enjoy it while you can. Soak up the sun. Slow down during the moments that matter.

If the pitch is close, swing the bat hard—you might just hit it. You're going to enjoy professional success; success isn't for the timid. Be calculated, but take chances. Don't leave your hard work up to an umpire's call. Be responsible for your own destiny.

You can't win alone, but you're surrounded by a great team; no amount of personal accomplishment is possible without them. People will leave your team—thank them for their time. People will join it—thank them every chance you get, and never minimize their contributions, however small. Remember, your accomplishments are their accomplishments too. Never take sole responsibility for an accomplishment, but always take sole responsibility for your failure.

One day, we all quit playing. You'll have to walk away from the game before long. We retire the numbers of great players to remember and honor their contributions. Be the type of person deserving of that honor. Be principled, guided by faith, kind, caring, understanding, present, and passionate. Let the doubts of others fuel your success. Most of all, leave a legacy you won't regret.

As a senior, I played my last baseball games. With the additions of Adam and Kevin to the team, 2003 was a family affair for Bismarck baseball. Playing with them was meaningful, but what we accomplished together was remarkable. The previous year, the team had only won two games; within twelve months, we improved that number to twenty-five, and won a district championship. District champions get their name on a banner that hangs in the gym at Bismarck High; the three of us ensured that, despite our name and the best efforts of the Bismarck natives, our hard work and determination would leave a legacy at that school.

That phenomenal season made it even harder to walk away from the game. To this day, the baseball field does something magical to me. No matter how bad things seem, stepping out of the dugout and onto the dirt immediately transforms me into a carefree eight-year-old. A professional career wouldn't have been unheard of in my family—a second cousin played for the Montreal Expos. But Bobby Henley was four inches taller than me and built like an Adonis. I was Bismarck High School good, but I would be kidding myself to think I was MLB good; baseball is a chaotic game, and there is no set trajectory to make it to the big leagues. I admitted to myself, begrudgingly, that I didn't have a future in professional baseball. So what was plan B? I had been offered opportunities to play for junior colleges, but they would leave very little time for academics—and my ambitions had grown on that front.

When my dad played ball, he wore a lot of different numbers. I was dead set on being my own person and creating my own path, so I intentionally chose a number that he never wore: the number 17. That number has always held a special meaning in my life, and even today I'm overcome with emotion watching my own children take the field with my last name and jersey number on their backs, a choice they have made to honor our bond.

My dad was seventeen when I was born; I was seventeen when Amanda and I got together; and at age seventeen, I resolved to make a sacrifice for a different way of life. I could have easily inherited Rand Auto Sales and continued the exploitative business my grandfather created. Even more easily, I could have become a racetrack junkie, shirking the responsibilities of mainstream society. Instead, I was determined to rise above the moral stains on my family. I wanted to be different. I wanted to become a lawyer—a profession focused on operating within the law, not on the crooked fringe of ethical acceptability.

HUNGRY AGAIN

The Gifted Program at my high school had been neglected through the years, and by the time I was starting my junior year it was barely breathing. In an effort to resuscitate the project, the school named a new director: Patti Pinkley, the woman that had recognized that I would benefit from special education as an elementary school student. Even after my behavioral troubles, Mrs. Pinkley felt that something inside of me was worth redeeming, and took me under her wing. She knew that I needed guidance academically, behaviorally, and psychologically, and she conducted the train that carried me far from my struggles in Bismarck.

Patti convinced me to take classes that she offered through the revitalized Gifted Program. For the next two years, for three hours a day, I worked with Mrs. Pinkley. The program allowed me to separate myself from the monotony of regular classes and remove myself from the watchful gaze of the principal, Mr. Milner. Each day, Mrs. Pinkley and I talked about my goals. We discussed how to apply to colleges, and how to manage the financial burdens higher education would bring. She promised me that we would find a way to make it work. I promised her I would do whatever it took.

She helped me write essays, apply for scholarships, fill out applications, and get the application fees waived. One day, late in the fall of 2002 during my senior year of high school, the phone rang in Mrs. Pinkley's classroom. She answered, "Mrs. Pinkley's room. Yes, it is. He is right here." She looked at me with a familiar expression, one that she often made when she was aggravated. She pointed toward me and advised, "It's for you."

My thoughts began to race—I knew these types of calls typically came from Mr. Milner's office. What had I done this time? Nothing came to mind, but that only made me more perplexed. Reluctantly, I answered the telephone, "Hello? This is Mike." An immediate reply did not follow, and my anticipation built. After a brief pause, I realized that the call was on hold, and that I needed to hit a button before I could answer.

I tried again, "Hello, this is Mike Randazzo." This time, a response came from a voice that I did not recognize. "Hello, Mr. Randazzo. This is Todd Taylor. I am an admissions counselor for the Pierre Laclede Honors College at the University of Missouri in St. Louis. I have some exciting news." As I listened, Mrs. Pinkley cracked a smile, and the tension eased out of my body. The conversation continued: I had received a full-tuition academic scholarship to the University of Missouri St. Louis. This was my chance. We had both kept our word.

A couple of things were clear: first, I wouldn't be getting any financial help from my family. Up until then, no one in my family had even graduated high school. College would have to be my thing. Second, I couldn't afford an apartment or dorm near campus, so I'd have to commute. On good days, the hour-and-a-half drive each way was doable. On bad days, it was a nightmare. Finally, I'd have work to afford gas.

To make it work, I made a deal with Grandpa Nick. He'd pay me $20 per day plus commission at the car lot. I scheduled Tuesday, Thursday, and Saturday shifts to earn the $60 needed for gas to drive to St. Louis three days a week. I hadn't had to worry about money for a while, but now, like in my early years, I had to figure out how to get by with very little. No extra money meant no hanging out with friends. Sometimes, it meant leaving home before sunrise with nothing but a water bottle, attending a full day of class, and then returning home after dark. An empty stomach and a lonely commute often made me question if the sacrifices were worth it, or even sustainable. But somehow, even in that environment of deprivation, I thrived.

As a freshman, I had no college credit—we had not been allowed to enroll in college courses or earn AP credits at Bismarck High. My scholarship covered as many classes and books as I wanted to take each semester, so I loaded up on credits—because I was commuting, this schedule would save time and money.

The financial benefits were enticing, but the workload was difficult to juggle. One semester, I took eighteen credit hours; another, I took twenty-four. My grades might have been better with fewer classes, but I graduated in two years and nine months—a year and three months early. But higher education wasn't my only major life change at this time.

WHAT ARE YOU PROPOSING?

By now, Amanda and I had moved in together. Jacob, Amanda, and I were a family. I knew that meant I would be foregoing the normal exploratory phase of college and young adulthood, but I didn't care. Amanda was everything I wanted and more. In the fall of 2003, I knew it was time to take the next step. I borrowed money from Grandpa Nick and found the nicest ring $250 could buy, hoping the sentiment would be more important than the quality of the jewelry sealing our future. Amanda deserved a grand gesture, a stage to shine on, and this proposal would erase the scarlet letter of her past.

I had the perfect plan. My mom still worked in the racing office, and had the connections with operations and track officials I would need to pull my scheme off—but I was hesitant to ask her for help. Mom and Amanda weren't necessarily fans of each other. Mom insisted on giving advice, and Amanda insisted on ignoring it. They each did what they thought was best for me. Often, their disagreements were about timing and procedure rather than results. Amanda fought to become the primary woman in my life, and Mom wouldn't easily cede that position.

My discussion with Mom about marrying Amanda would be my first closing argument. Mom worried about me finishing college, knowing Amanda had responsibilities that didn't align with college and career aspirations—she knew I would quit school to support my family if they needed me to. I assured her I'd finish college. Unconvinced but appeased, she blessed the plan and became my co-conspirator.

I planned to lure Amanda to Fairmount Park, saying that our racehorse, Table the Motion, would be honored with a race named after her. We planned to meet at the Winner's Circle, the small area where owners, trainers, friends, and fans take a picture with the jockey and winning horse, after the fifth race. I needed her to believe we would be there for something ceremonious.

Due to the deep link between horseracing and gambling, each track is connected to the others through live video feeds called simulcasts, allowing fans worldwide to watch and bet on live races. The network boasted over one million viewers. Before the fifth race, Mom told me track officials would include the proposal in the simulcast. The whole racing world would be watching.

I was nervous all evening. After the fifth race, I felt like throwing up. Our group walked toward the Winner's Circle with Amanda. We were admitted, and everyone circled around as we always did after winning a race. Trembling, I listened for my cue. The track announcer's deep voice echoed through the stadium: "Can I direct your attention to the Winner's Circle for a special presentation?"

The racing crowd, my guests, and the simulcast audience watched as I walked Amanda to the center of the circle. I was desperate to be rid of the burden of the ring—this was my Frodo Baggins moment. I reached into my pocket, removed the token of my devotion, and knelt. Amanda's hands flew to her mouth. Shaking, I asked, "Will you marry me?" A camera flash commemorated the moment she nodded yes. I took my own mental snapshot of the celebration; I wanted to forever remember the happiness of that day and the pedestal I was permitted to place my future wife upon. "She said yes!" the announcer proclaimed over the loudspeaker.

We married on March 19, 2005. Conscientious of our tight budget, we planned the perfect wedding—or, I should say, Amanda planned because the perfect wedding, because I did little more than agree with her. Our families pitched in to make the reception happen. On a budget of about $3,500, Amanda found a dress, rented a venue, decorated, got her hair done, created and mailed invitations, secured a DJ, provided 200 guests with a meal, and paid for a cake. Making the most of what we had became the marching orders of our marriage.

BABY BLUES

Soon after we married, we discussed having our first child. Jacob was six and in school, and Amanda was free to pursue pregnancy again—on her own terms, this time. Undeterred by the failing relationships around us, we decided that waiting until after I finished school would be a poor choice. Amanda stopped taking birth control, and soon after, she conceived.

Watching my wife's body change was challenging—not because I found her less attractive, but because I watched ordinary tasks become a struggle. Amanda has always been a doer, and I was used to seeing her overcome adversity. Convincing her to slow down was the greatest struggle of her pregnancy, and more generally, our marriage.

While my marriage flourished, my parents' continued to fall apart. I seldom saw Dad. Rejection by her partner led Mom into a deep depression. She took multiple jobs to stay physically close to the man who had emotionally quit the marriage. Whether it was in drugs or women, Dad sought pleasure elsewhere. Both neglected Kevin as they played an emotional game of freeze tag, each stuck in place by heartbreak or heartlessness, trying to ensure the other didn't move on.

Although surrounded by disorder, my marriage was somehow shielded from discontent. I jubilantly called every friend and relative to announce Amanda was pregnant. As we planned to expand our family, an unexpected declaration came from my absent father, through Grandpa Nick. Before my excitement about becoming a biological father had worn off, Grandpa Nick broke the news: Dad had impregnated a woman who worked at the racetrack, a woman I'd never met. She'd give birth to my second brother.

Eighteen years later, I still feel a tinge of disdain that my moment was stolen. I'm terribly sorry for the years it took to understand that my brother Dustin was in no way responsible for the circumstances of his birth. While I viewed his mother as a homewrecker, my parents' marriage was already on the rocks. Unable to tolerate his illegitimate activities any longer, Mom broke away from Dad, and in most cases that would have been the end of it: Dad would have moved on to be a present father in his child's life, a spouse to Dustin's mom, and they would have made their relationship work for his benefit. Mom would have found someone more appreciative, someone she could trust to follow laws and sacred vows. But Dustin wasn't the end of their marriage. Before they reunited, however, things would get much worse.

Right before Amanda and I married, Grandpa Nick co-signed a loan for a small, used, double-wide trailer. Grandpa let us put our trailer on the Randazzo property outside Bismarck city limits, which now held three houses. Grandpa Nick and Grandma Janelle lived in the blue split-level at the end of the drive, Mom lived in the yellow split-level in the middle, and Amanda, Jacob, and I lived in the small trailer at the front.

Not long after we found out that Dustin and my son would be coming in the spring, Dad's illicit activities came to a head. Jorge, Christina, and thirty-four other members of the Garcia-Serna Cartel were indicted on federal charges, including money laundering and drug trafficking. Knowing an arrest warrant had been signed, Christina and Jorge fled to Mexico to escape justice. Dad no longer had a connection or the desire to continue his criminal activities. He didn't know if he'd be implicated in the operation, and until he knew more, he would return to Bismarck to hide. But hiding out proved to be difficult with a pregnant girlfriend. Taking what money he could, Dad purchased a camping trailer, pulled it to the front yard of the house he used to share with Mom, and connected it to her electric grid. In front of the house he formerly shared with his wife, he hid from the federal government with his pregnant mistress.

Dad had returned to claim what he had abandoned. His unexpected presence was bittersweet: I desperately wanted him near, but despised the baggage he brought. Watching the man she had married bring his indiscretion quite literally into her front yard had so mentally drained Mom that even the birth of her first biological grandchild was not enough to tip her psychological scales to the positive. After a few days of seeing her unwanted front yard neighbors, she left her home. For the first time in my life, Mom and I didn't live in the same house or right next to each other.

Born almost exactly one month apart, Dustin and Michael Jr. (Joey) marked the arrival of a new generation of Randazzo boys. Due to the timing of their births, I knew that Joey would always struggle to escape constant comparison to the milestones and accomplishments of his uncle. Nevertheless, they would become each other's best friends.

After half a day in labor and multiple failed epidurals, Joey arrived with curiosity, looking around and soaking in his new surroundings without a sound. A few times in life, we can feel the world change: the earth stands still, and our cosmic course is forever rerouted. Joey's birth was one such moment. As I held him, I promised things would be different for him than they had been for me.

TO PROTECT AND SERVE

I need to highlight the sacrifices Amanda made for our family. After Joey had arrived and I had graduated from college, Amanda and I made a pact: she'd work to pay the bills, and I'd focus on law school. On a whim, Amanda decided to go through the law enforcement academy with my brother Kevin. Kevin convinced her it was the fastest way to get college credits and her degree. In the year between my graduation and law school, Amanda focused on her own education for the first time. Upon graduating from the academy, she immediately became a Sheriff's Deputy. What had started as a whim became a career that has lasted nearly two decades. She's still a police officer today.

Being married to a police officer is not easy. Each day, you watch your spouse leave home knowing they will face countless unknown dangers while trying to help people. There's nothing more comforting than the sound of their vests' Velcro straps being unfastened—the sure sign that they're home safe. As a police officer, Amanda sacrificed her mental and physical health to support my ambitions.

Law enforcement then, and even more so now, was a distinctly male profession, known for its military discipline and look. The prototypical officer was a large, burly man—on a good day, wearing heels, Amanda is 5'2" and 120 pounds. If partners were chosen based on looks alone, she'd probably be coming off the bench. But criminals would be advised not to judge a book by its cover.

Upon completing the academy, Amanda immediately sought a job, applying to every department within driving distance. Many refused her even a courtesy interview. They told her she was too small to succeed. Undeterred, she continued to apply, and continued to be rejected. Her search led her to a department with a history of misconduct, one just looking for warm bodies until a new administration took over—but she was desperate for a job. After her interview, I received a call from the department.

The sergeant introduced himself, said he'd interviewed Amanda, and wanted to discuss her potential employment with me before making an offer. Apparently, they wanted my permission for my wife to work there, ensuring I was on board with her working with potentially crude men. I thought that this paternalism was disrespectful to Amanda's hard work and self-worth. While societal norms had changed, law enforcement was stuck in the 1960s. This request set the tone for her next two decades of work in the police department, but those stories are hers to tell. Out of respect for her, let's just say sexual advances, harassment, and discrimination were constant, and came more commonly from co-workers than from perpetrators.

As off-color as the sergeant's gesture seemed, law school was looming, and we had two kids to provide for. Amanda called back and accepted the job. All the department could promise was a year-long contract, ending when a new sheriff would take over. Amanda had to prove herself under those precarious conditions. Fortunately, she got many chances, and rose to the occasion—but uncertainty still shrouded our future as she waited to see if the new sheriff would keep her.

In the little time she had, Amanda thrived. She expertly de-escalated volatile situations, as her less-than-intimidating stature relaxed armed suspects ready to meet aggressive challengers with force. Unbeknownst to her, the incoming sheriff noticed her successes. He not only kept her on staff, but he also gave her a clear path to advancement. Knowing we'd be financially solvent solidified my ability to focus on and complete law school. Law school would bring a new set of challenges, but my success would not have been possible without her sacrifice.

OUTLAW AT THE SCHOOL OF LAW

Knowing my criminology and criminal justice degree would provide only enough to scrape by, I had to take the next step. Because of the rigorous pace of my undergrad education, I didn't feel prepared to start law school in 2006. I decided to take a gap year, and used my criminology degree to work as a child abuse and neglect investigator for the state of Missouri. The job paid the bills, but left me displeased and emotionally distant. My coworkers were wonderful, but the horrible crimes we investigated caused a profound mental anguish, the kind that can lead to depression and addiction. While I didn't turn to substances, I became more determined than ever to become a lawyer.

While working as an investigator, I compiled reference letters, took the Law School Admissions Test, and applied to schools in the St. Louis area. With two kids and a wife, we were anchored near Bismarck—everything meaningful was there. If I had to choose between staying nearby and attending a distant law school, I wouldn't have moved. Luckily, I was accepted into Saint Louis University's School of Law. I knew I could commute, having done so for my undergrad.

In the fall of 2007, I attended my first class at SLU Law. I would quickly learn that law school was like learning a foreign language. The Latin maxims weren't the issue; legal writing was. I'd written papers in undergrad, but this was different. My first assignment was to research and write a legal brief, just like I'd have to do as a lawyer. To be honest, I'd never read a legal brief or opinion before. The formatting and rhetoric were completely alien to me. Day after day, I researched and wrote, putting in extra effort to crack this legal code. The day I turned in the brief, I felt relief and optimism, proud to have completed a real lawyer task.

During the next class, I eagerly awaited my grade and feedback. My professor handed back my masterpiece with excessive red marks and a large D+ circled at the top, with instructions to see her after class. In law school, anything below a C is failing. If you fail two classes, you're kicked out. I was weeks into law school and already unable to stay afloat. My stomach sank as the minutes ticked by, bringing my date with defeat ever closer.

I stood in the hall outside her office and knocked lightly, hoping she wouldn't hear—if she didn't, I could say I tried to meet but missed her. Somehow, she heard my weak rapping and asked, "Is someone there?" The dryness in my mouth and lump in my throat made it impossible to respond. She approached the door to investigate.

As the door swung open, we made eye contact. She invited me in. She sat at her desk, and I followed suit. She broke the silence with frank dialogue: "Mr. Randazzo, your brief was extremely poorly written. I could tell you didn't spend much time researching, preparing, or writing it. It's apparent you don't belong here. Don't waste your time; you're not lawyer material. Find something else to do."

I put my head down and reflected in silence. I mumbled that I had spent many hours preparing and had given the paper my best effort. "I assumed you'd say that," she replied, "and if that's true, I'm even more concerned about your ability to pass. My job is to prepare law students to be lawyers, and I don't see that career happening for you."

I left the office and closed the door as she'd instructed. I stood in the hallway and tried to process what was happening. I'd experienced failure before, but never in school. The conversation echoed in my brain as a life-changing decision loomed. Convinced there was no alternative, I decided to drop out.

After reaching that decision, I sat in the hallway to ponder my next steps. For what seemed like hours, I just sat there, unable to come to terms with this type of incompetence. In the hallway of this Jesuit institution, I was compelled to prayer. I'd never been the type to pray—Grandma Janelle had introduced me to God, but the details were fuzzy, and other than a quick grace before meals, the big man and I were strangers. With my buttocks firmly on the ground, my knees folded like a triangle, and my face in my hands, I asked God for guidance, clarity, and direction. What happened next is hard to interpret as anything but divine intervention.

Upon opening my eyes, I saw a corkboard littered with announcements. The usual student bulletins were there, along with event and guest speaker advertisements. My attention was drawn to a flyer for a defense attorney's speaking engagement that afternoon. I decided to attend, hoping to get one final benefit of being a law student, even if I'd never be a lawyer.

Entering the lecture hall, I expected to hear about the famous cases he'd worked or crazy stories he had experienced. Instead, he gave a speech that could have been meant solely for me. He spoke about the legal profession's exclusivity, how he had failed out of law school on his first attempt, and how he had never been the trust-fund type that law schools desire. He explained how the profession needed diverse people doing the job for the right reasons. He impressed upon us that our personal circumstances separated us, but also brought common purposes to our lives. Ultimately, he compared our experiences to a $2 bill—unique, but no less valuable. Underneath each seat, he had planted just such a $2 bill in an envelope. I still possess that bill; when I feel lost, I hold it in my hands and reconnect to its meaning.

After the speech, I reset my mind and approach. Determined to finish the semester before evaluating my desire to continue, I worked as hard as I could. I spent every waking moment driving to class, in class, in the library, or studying, neglecting all of the normal duties of a husband and father. Amanda picked up the slack and, even though she worked, she still handled most of the household duties alone. Although Mom was no longer living next door, she helped with childcare for Joey and Jacob, coming to my house to babysit or taking the boys with her to the apartment she rented near her job in Collinsville.

For the next three years, I focused every ounce of effort I had into school, and my renewed dedication started to pay off. I passed that writing class with a C. Each semester, I did a little better, earning mostly Cs my first year, then mostly Bs, and finally all As and Bs my third year. Ultimately, I graduated in the top half of my class.

Wanting to get into the courtroom quickly, I became certified through the Missouri Supreme Court to practice as a Rule 13 law student. Rule 13 allowed a student who completed three semesters to, under the supervision of a licensed attorney, handle cases like a fully-certified lawyer. But finding an attorney willing to be responsible for me was a problem. I had no connections, so I started cold-calling lawyers. After exhausting the defense lawyers, I called county prosecuting attorneys' offices to volunteer in exchange for courtroom experience.

Eventually, the cold calls led to an opportunity. After calling the Iron County Prosecuting Attorney, the man I spoke with invited me for an interview. I met Robert "Scott" Killen in Ironton, Missouri. While Scott did not know me, he knew my last name. Scott made a big first impression. He was exceptionally large, food being his vice. Although ridiculed for his obesity, Scott was a brilliant legal scholar and the kindest soul I'd ever met. Scott invested in me, despite my unconventional history.

Our tag team worked well: Scott was the brain, and I was his courtroom presence. I gained invaluable experience as a lawyer with him—there was no better person to learn from than R. Scott Killen. Scott introduced me to judges and lawyers, and used his keys to open doors I never should have been allowed through. I can never repay his kindness and willingness to help an undeserving kid.

After I graduated, the Missouri Bar Exam blocked my path. Most students spend the few months after completing law school in commercial bar exam review courses that teach you how to take the test and what to expect—but they're expensive. I didn't have the several hundred dollars required, so I studied independently. A recently licensed attorney I met through Scott Killen learned of my struggles and let me borrow his law review books. Equipped with these books and the outlines of my classes, I embarked on the greatest study session of my life: two calendar months straight of daily, tireless work. The costs of taking the exam and booking the necessary hotel stay for the two days of testing meant that I would only get one shot to pass the test.

As a reward for graduating from law school, my family took a vacation to Fort Morgan, Alabama. I felt like I was drowning under my studies, and the trip was supposed to give me some relief from that suffocating pressure. Unfortunately, I would end up having to save someone else from drowning—literally.

HOW TO SAVE A LIFE

Compounding the stress of my studies, Amanda announced in January of 2010 that she was pregnant with our final child. We had never actually agreed it was time to try for another, but Amanda had decided to discontinue her birth-control regimen. She was ready for another baby, but for me the timing could not have been more challenging. By the time of my graduation, her belly had expanded, and she was beginning to suffer from pregnancy-related high blood pressure. Those complications caused her to take a leave from her job. The next few transitional months would bring about changes that would shape my life.

Until I was in my late twenties, our few family vacations always brought us to the white sandy beaches of southeastern Alabama or northwestern Florida. When the Carlot or his criminal rackets were doing well enough to make some extra money, Grandpa would make sure to put aside enough to rent a large home right on the beach for a few days. Everyone was invited, and usually, everyone would go. Grandpa Nick felt deeply content there: watching his olive skin turn to deep walnut was worth the eleven-hour car trip to the coast. We all enjoyed the water, but I believe Grandpa's soul had been baptized in the briny pools that tranquilly flattened the sand and temporarily eased his mind. Although the gains paying for them may have been ill-gotten, I was thankful that we were able to take a few of these trips together. The last of them was the most eventful.

Standing on the beach and staring out into the vast expanse of the ocean can make one feel insignificant. Fighting the might of the waves can humble even the proudest warrior. Appropriately, one of the instances in my life in which I most powerfully felt God's supernatural strength occurred on the seashore.

During the long drive from Missouri, Amanda and I discussed our goals for the trip. She wanted to relax as much as possible so that her blood pressure wouldn't force a premature birth. I wanted to be able to study in peace, and I couldn't think of a better place to do that than in the warm sand near the gulf. A final mutual goal was to have this one last family event before we had to start pulling an extra chair up to our table of four.

We arrived late that afternoon as the sun was close to setting. Grandma Janelle, Grandpa Nick, Dawn, Mom, Dad, Kevin, Kevin's wife Treasure, Amanda, Jacob, Joey, and I all settled in one side of a three-story duplex. We had never stayed at this house before, and the other side of the house appeared to already be occupied. We unpacked and then raced to the beach. As we walked down the shore, I noticed that we were in a very secluded area. There were no lifeguards, no beach patrol—very few beachgoers whatsoever.

The only other people we saw were a group of women ranging in age from about twenty years old to sixty. That group of women turned out to be our neighbors in the duplex. My attention was immediately drawn to the youngest of them, who seemed to be having the time of her life. It was apparent, most notably from her infectious laugh and genuine excitement, that this woman had Down syndrome. I surreptitiously listened in on the conversation the women were having. The youngest of the bunch was celebrating a birthday, and her wish was to see the ocean. They had been unable to afford the trip until now, and their uncontained joy spread to Amanda and me. We watched the family walk up and down the beach, dipping their toes into the water or getting drenched as large waves crashed into the beach at just the right angle. The group had no worldly riches, but they appeared to be spiritually wealthy. Their family shared little resemblance to ours, but what would happen on that beach would connect us forever.

My inadvertent spying yielded some additional information about their family. The group was only there for weekend. Their goal was to get into the water for a picture at some point, but the youngest could not swim. She was instructed never to get in deeper than her waist. I watched as she walked out a bit with her hand extended forward above the waves to ensure she was not getting in too deep.

The typical daydream of the beach conjures sunshine, warm weather, and calm, rhythmic waves. The second day in Fort Morgan was more like a nightmare. Rain, fog, and strong winds relegated us to the confines of the duplex. The nasty weather brought with it specific swimming warnings. The warning system was rather easy to understand: a yellow flag indicated that some caution was needed, but it was generally safe to swim; a red flag warned that there were strong currents, and that swimming could be hazardous; and a double red flag closed the beach. Entry into the water during a double red flag was punishable as a criminal offense. On our second day, a double red flag rippled in the heavy wind.

At this time, I was twenty-five years old, and a lifeguard-trained swimmer. Even though I was confident in my ability to stay afloat, I would have only dared to enter that surf if it meant life or death. On that fateful day, it did. About midday, as the entire family searched for something non-beach-related to do, a frantic scream echoed through our building from outside: "HELP!"

The voice was unfamiliar, but the tone was unmistakable: someone was in distress. Kevin and I raced to the ocean-facing side of the duplex to investigate. As we scanned the water, I recognized the source of the shouting: the mother of the disabled woman. As she continued to hysterically yell for help, she pointed farther into the roaring ocean.

Without further thought, Kevin and I sprang into action. The rain had hardened the sand, which made running through the dunes much easier than it would have been on a dry day. In no time, we reached the mother and tried to get as much information in as little time as possible. We quickly ascertained that the woman with Down syndrome and her aunt had been sucked into the deep water without warning. The woman advised that the aunt was competent swimmer, but that neither herself nor her daughter could swim.

We continued to scan the water, but found no signs of life. The massive waves obstructed our sightlines for seconds at a time, and would then violently crash as they made landfall. Finally, between the waves, I noticed a head bob out of the water and gasp for air. Kevin saw the same. A quick look was all we needed to know the mission ahead. We hurriedly combed the beach to find any floatation assistance we could, and then, armed with a boogie board and a pool noodle, we marched toward our battle with nature.

Unbeknownst to us, another member of the other group had called the authorities for assistance. Just before entering the water, two first response units pulled directly onto the beach. Kevin and I relaxed, relieved that professionals were now on the scene. That relief was short-lived. One emergency responder explained, "We cannot go into the water. It is a double red flag. It is not safe for us or anyone else."

We were flabbergasted. I thought to myself, "They are going to let these women die." A quick glance back at Kevin revealed he was thinking the same thing. As our eyes connected, so did our brains. Without a word, we sprang back to action.

As we entered the water, a yell from a loudspeaker echoed across the beach: "Don't get in the water. It is a double red flag. You will be arrested." The warning didn't stop us—on this day, the Brothers Randazzo would not be deterred by threats of arrest.

As soon as the first wave broke near my feet, I was knocked off balance and fell face-forward into the quickly receding riptide. As I attempted to stand, I was knocked off balance again. Keeping my eye on the helpless struggling woman, I was finally able to begin swimming. Kevin, just a few inches behind me, and I attempted to close the ever-expanding gap between ourselves and the young lady. The harder we swam, the more exhausted we became, paddling tirelessly toward the spot where we had last seen her head emerge from the water.

Steadfast, we pushed on for what felt like hours, although in reality it must have been minutes at most. Soon, what began as a rescue operation turned into a fight for survival. I felt myself slip below the surface of the water and struggled to return to the surface to catch my breath. Our efforts to close the gap began to feel Sisyphean. Just before I decided to abandon the rescue, I saw auburn hair floating atop the water. I wrapped my arms around the woman and pulled her from beneath the surface. As her mouth reached the air, she gasped to refill her lungs. The struggle to stay afloat and breathe normally was my next focus.

The woman, who was quite large in stature, wrapped her entire body around mine, as if attempting to use me as a personal floatation device. She sank her fingernails deep into the flesh of my back, preventing me from keeping us buoyant. Remembering the little rescue training that I had, I rotated to my back—a move that likely saved both of our lives. It was easier to stay afloat in this position, but paddling the two of us backward against the pull of the riptide left me the most physically fatigued I have ever been.

Kevin and I transferred the woman back and forth, providing the other just enough time to catch their breath on the boogie board. The further we traveled with the woman in tow, the more exhausted we both became. I started to doubt that we would make it to shore. Just before I succumbed to exhaustion, my feet felt the familiar touch of the sandy bottom of the shallows. The depth of the water allowed me to stand. While the woman sobbed relentlessly, still clinging to me for life, I walked her to the shore and collapsed on the beach.

I awoke to a very perturbed and very pregnant Amanda. As a paramedic provided me with supplemental oxygen, the preceding events started to feel less heroic and more foolish. The remaining bystanders scolded me for breaking the law and swimming out to rescue the disabled woman in spite of their double red flag ordinance. Just as I remembered the other woman stranded in the water, I turned to see her being pulled back to the shore on a flotation device by Kevin, Dad, and a few others who had joined in to help. With much less of a struggle, she was safely returned to the beach.

Back on dry land, the second woman explained their predicament. "We were walking on the beach with our feet in the water when we were hit with a wave that knocked us both down. Before we could get up, we were swept out into water over our heads. I did everything I could to get to her, but I couldn't reach her. I just knew she had drowned. I floated on my back and prayed that we would somehow survive! When the firefighters didn't try to come out to save us, I was ready to give up hope. My prayers were answered when I saw you two spring into action!"

As ill-conceived as our plan was, it had worked. I often reflect upon the significance of that trip. The rescue could easily be written off as a coincidence—the right people, at the right time, in the right place. Or maybe, it was yet another picture that God had painted, with his servants as the brush. I hoped, deeply, that this event could be redemption for the sins of my forefathers. Could these actions atone for their misdeeds? Could any? Could our act of heroism be enough to liberate myself from our inherited mark of Cain?

DADDY'S GIRL?

Amanda dreamed of a little girl, one she could dress in frills and bows, who'd fancy soft and delicate things—unlike her two boys. During my last year of law school, Amanda was ready for another child. I wanted another, too, though the timing was debated. Just as Joey had arrived near my college graduation, Gracie came soon after law school, born the same week I took the Missouri Bar Exam. But her entry was different than Joey's—in fact, Gracie wasn't even Gracie for most of the pregnancy.

During our first ultrasound, the doctor drew a circle on the image and labeled it "schlong." I saw the disappointment in Amanda's face. We'd agreed this would be our last child, and we were having another boy. I also sensed that Amanda doubted the results. Soon, we discussed names, settling on Alexander Joseph, calling him Alex, Xander, or AJ. We jokingly considered Alexandria for a girl.

Months passed, and we had more imaging. The technician moved the paddle, measured things, and then said, "Your baby girl appears to be doing great." I looked at Amanda in disbelief. A bright smile and a tear affirmed that she'd heard it too.

A month before her due date, during a scheduled appointment, the doctor said the baby was coming that day. By now, we had a new name: Grace JoAnn Randazzo. It just seemed right. We chose "Grace" because of its Latin meaning, but her middle name was nuanced. Amanda's Aunt Nancy and sister Ladonna had the middle name Jo. My mom's middle name is Joan. Amanda's mom's middle name was Ann. My Grandma Sandy had the middle name Ann. JoAnn was an amalgamation of all those names and people.

Complications meant that Amanda would have to deliver by Cesarean section, unlike with the boys. As the baby was removed from Amanda, I heard a gulp, then a gargle, and then the most piercing scream. Gracie had entered the world in a very Gracie fashion.

Holding my daughter, I made her the same promise I made Joey: I would change our family's trajectory. She would have a chance to be herself, uninhibited by her inheritance of baggage.

BACK IN THE GAME

Walking off the baseball field in June 2003 felt like saying goodbye to my first love. Yearning to stay in the game, I started playing slow-pitch softball after graduating high school. Thought it never fully scratched the itch, softball provided respite from college, law school, law practice, and life.

I was never as good at softball as I was at baseball, but I became competent. I played third base and pitched. Fresh out of high school, a group of us local kids made a name for ourselves. I was first exposed to softball during my dad's playing days, and I now played with many of his era's greats, who still dominated the game. As they aged out, their spikes were filled by their children. A similar passing of the torch occurred for Dad, Kevin, Adam, and me. For a few years, we shared the field. I don't think I ever played a game without Kevin or Adam. It was our thing. Sometimes, when Dad wasn't distracted, he'd play too. He was a forty-year-old playing against youngsters half his age, but his skills were still serviceable.

Our team was named the Indians out of nostalgia and homage to our Bismarck High School mascot. Grandpa Nick was our coach, always included. He came with us to tournaments, barking unrealistic orders. He didn't know the game or the rules, but he motivated people. If nothing else, he was a convenient scapegoat for Adam and me to blame for any bad line-up changes. As always, his broad shoulders could carry whatever load we burdened him with, and he thrived in his role.

Because of Dad's longevity and our closeness, we won multiple softball championships, including local and state titles. We even made deep runs in World Series tournaments, though we never won. Tournaments brought accolades, and while I didn't play for acknowledgment, it was nice to hear my name called. I made several all-tournament teams, and was even named MVP once at the 2011 Missouri State Tournament. That tournament was special.

Knowing the kids were getting older and career demands were increasing, I had announced that 2011 would be my last year. Because it was my last ride, we wanted our best product on the field. Over the years, we had been lucky enough to retain some talented old players and pick up some amazing new ones. That mix created the best team I have ever been a part of.

Over the years, men's slow-pitch softball had started to become exactly what I was trying to escape. Evenings and weekends away from work would be spent dealing with conflict, hearing grown men regress to childhood and throw temper tantrums when the breaks didn't go their way. Winning was fun, but the game became contaminated by a win-at-all-costs mentality. Steroids, altered bats, and targeting to injure other players became accepted. When it was time to walk away from the game, it was easier than I thought it would be—but I did get one last shot at glory.

By now, I pitched full-time—third base was reserved for stronger players. A slow-pitcher delivers the softball underhand. Because the speed is limited, pitch placement and movement separate good from great. The position was my only chance to play in the field, so I worked hard to control the pitch location. According to league standards, the pitcher's mound lies exactly fifty feet from the batter's box. Within the batter's box usually stands a brawny alpha-male carrying a bat designed to turn balls into 100-miles-per-hour missiles. In essence, the pitcher is a sitting duck. After years of serious injuries and deaths suffered by unlucky pitchers whose instincts were not fast enough to dodge bullets from the batter's box, today's game has standardized protective equipment for pitchers, including helmets, chest protectors, and shin-guards. In my twenties, those developments had not occurred—but my desire to play the game outweighed my sound judgment.

That final year culminated in one last Missouri state championship. Confident we'd win, the five Randazzo men made the trip to Jefferson City. Roles were defined: Kevin, a lanky lefty, played first base. I'd pitch. Adam, healing from a broken wrist, slipped off his cast and took some at-bats. Dad was there for pitching relief, welcomed in the Missouri heat. Grandpa's health prevented him from standing or staying out in the heat, but he came along anyways for moral support and a final coaching stint. I knew this would be our last ride, and I tried to soak it all in.

The details of the games escape me, but the feelings are engrained in my heart. Dad played a stabilizing, supportive role. He calmed me when I was aggravated and encouraged me when I needed a boost. I repeatedly snagged hard-hit line drives. That weekend was my peak. I was transformed back to my twelve-year-old self. Dad and Grandpa were my heroes, and I shared the field with my brothers. The results were secondary, but we went undefeated and became state champions for the last time. After a team vote, I was named MVP. I knew I'd played well, but I hadn't even considered personal accolades, too distracted by the knowledge that it was the last time I would play with Dad and Grandpa.

That generational passing of the torch and my subsequent retirement didn't stop me from yearning for the game. Soon, I'd be back, but my role would be different. With my playing career over and the kids growing up, I humbly accepted my new position: coach.

Coaching provided the mental vacation from being a trial attorney that I needed. Sharing the proper way to play the game was slightly less fulfilling than playing it myself, but the opportunity allowed sports to still play a role in my life. Just as in my relationship to my own dad, some of my most cherished moments as a parent have occurred on the playing field. The accomplishments of my children and their teams are certainly praiseworthy, but they are not my stories to tell. I am just thankful to have been a part of those journeys for the last couple of decades. As the kids age, other than some one-on-one training, I have been relegated to the stands. Being shushed by an umpire just doesn't feel the same from the bleachers. From player to coach to cheerleader, it has been a monumental struggle to accept my fate. A huge portion of my life has been dedicated to athletics, and I am so grateful to have had the privilege.

INDEFENSIBLE

My dream had always been to go to law school, become a defense attorney, and buck the system. I grew up viewing the legal system as oppressive to poor people like me and overly permissive to the rich, regardless of how they obtained their money. To that end, fresh out of law school, I took a job as a public defender. I felt comfortable there: when I interned at the Iron County Prosecuting Attorney's office, I got to work with many of the attorneys who would now be my colleagues. Excited to get into court, I accepted the position and began the paid portion of my career as a defense attorney.

The attorneys that worked for the Missouri State Public Defender's Farmington office were, then and still to this day, some of the most skilled litigators in our entire court system. I hoped to absorb some of their courtroom skills through observation or osmosis. Some of those skills must have sunk in, as the foundation and training I received as a public defender made me a litigator. More than anything, I took away from that job an appreciation for what public defenders are required to do.

The details of the job are seldom understood. Under the United States Constitution, those charged with a crime are guaranteed a right to an attorney, even if they cannot afford one. Each state is left to develop its own system to appoint attorneys to represent poor people and ensure that the constitutional right to an attorney is not violated. Very few have the honor and courage it takes to accept that role. Compared to attorneys in private practice, public defenders make very little money. They don't get to choose who they fight for—a public defender must accept the appointment of the court and ethically represent their clients, regardless of how reprehensible their allegations. Most of the people that public defenders represent are guilty of the crime that they have been charged with. As a result, a public defender must get comfortable with going against long odds. Losing is part of the culture, but losing gracefully is an art.

The job is even more trying in rural areas. Poor people seldom have reliable telephone numbers or home addresses. They lack the resources to get to and from court and office meetings. In rural America, public transportation does not exist—there are no buses, taxis, or trains to carry people long distances. For a public defender, maintaining even basic contact with your client is a struggle. Because the rural Missouri contains some of the poorest regions in the country, most of the criminal defendants in our courts qualify for and are represented by public defenders.

Those harsh conditions, however, were not what forced me to make a change. While working as a defense attorney, I always focused on rights. I viewed myself not as defending a specific person or their actions, but as defending their rights under the Constitution. For some time, that mindset allowed me to set aside the horrific acts of murderers, rapists, and abusers. But it took only one case to change my perspective, a change that would alter the path of my career.

The image is seared into my memory: a nine-year-old boy, bound to a chair with duct tape, socks stuffed into his mouth to silence his screams. That case was the moment I knew I could no longer be a public defender.

I was forced to represent a man who, over about twelve hours, had committed horrific acts against his grandchild. It was New Year's Eve, and my client went to a party at his grandchild's home. He was supposed to keep an eye on the boy, but he deemed that responsibility too great an inconvenience; my client was worried that meeting the child's basic needs would ruin his good time. Removing the child from his presence for the next day was his solution. Once the kid was out of the picture, the alcohol could flow, and methamphetamine could be used freely. The man forced his grandchild into a straitjacket, the kind Hannibal Lecter is confined with in *Silence of the Lambs*: a white canvas garment fastened tight with leather straps and metal buckles. He tied his grandson's feet together with duct tape, and then taped him into an office chair. To ensure that the boy's protestations wouldn't be heard, the man balled up a pair of socks and stuffed them into his mouth. Then he wound duct tape all around his head, sealing the boy's lips closed and tightly wrapping the tape around his hair.

The child was left in that condition for at least eighteen hours. When he was discovered, he was in a horrible state. His body was limp, the straitjacket wet with tears and involuntary urination. Why? Why would someone entrusted with the care of a child do such a thing? The most common answer is selfishness. The group had their rager while the child suffered in a bedroom, out of sight and out of mind, until the next day. It was a New Year's Day miracle that the child had not suffocated during the night.

The man insisted that we take the case to trial. I knew that his callous demeanor would not play well in front of a jury, but it was not my decision. I prepared as best as I could, and we had a trial. I argued that there was no manual for raising a child and that he was doing the best he could as a grandfather. I argued, with a straight face, that the child had behaviors like ADHD that made the restraints necessary. I even argued that my client was sorry for what he did, which he was not.

I remember how dirty my family's car used to get as we traveled the gravel roads of my childhood—so dirty that at times I couldn't see out of the windows. I felt that dirty representing this man; dirty enough that I could I longer see where I was headed, like my soul had somehow been covered in grime, obstructing my vision of what I wanted to be.

After deliberating for less than ten minutes, the jury returned a guilty verdict. I was relieved. I was relieved that the jury didn't buy my bullshit. It was the only time in my life that I was satisfied to lose.

After making my way home that evening, instead of reaching for some substance to numb my brain, I silently watched my children playing, oblivious to the dangers of the world outside. I wrestled with myself over the reality that if I had done my job a little better, I would have made my own children less safe by letting a bad man walk free. Eventually, those dirty windows became clearer, and I knew I could no longer be a public defender. My feeling of satisfaction that my client was going to prison reaffirmed this conclusion. If I were going to be a criminal litigator, I would have to be a prosecuting attorney—a role that I would not just enjoy, but thrive in.

Representing the state of Missouri was a highlight of my career. I tried a lot of cases as a prosecuting attorney. My job allowed me to be a conscientious litigator—and more importantly, I got to make my own children a little safer by locking up the bad guys.

THE ALPHA-GAL

My greatest fear is that my brain will lose its ability to make sense of the world; that my sense of reality will be altered in such a way that my memories become corrupted. Life only matters because of the specifics of those memories; erasing them erases me. Mental infirmity has always existed in my life. Grandpa Nick suffered from depression and bipolar disorder. Dad presents bipolar and depressive symptoms like Grandpa Nick, with substance use disorder sprinkled on top. Mom has depression and post-traumatic stress disorder. As for me, I have been cursed with debilitating anxiety.

I spent almost every minute with my mom from my birth until I began school, and I remember severely struggling with worry and anxiety when I had to leave her to begin the Head Start Program. On Sunday, Monday, Tuesday, Wednesday, and Thursday evenings, I struggled to go to sleep because I knew the next morning meant we would be separated once again. Once at school, I would gradually recover and settle in with the other children—but after lunch, a new fear would always set in. Every afternoon, I worried that Mom was not going to pick me up, that she had somehow forgotten me, and that I was going to be left to fend for myself. I would stare out the window each day, paralyzed by this unfounded and ridiculous fear. I still don't understand the genesis of those worries. Most likely, I was afflicted with the unofficial disorder of Momma's Boy's Anxiety.

Starting kindergarten did nothing to alleviate these feelings and behaviors. The cycle of evening dread and afternoon fear dominated my adolescence. Eventually, the thoughts in my head became manifested in nervous tics. Habitually, I would shrug my shoulders up toward my head, and then push my left shoulder forward. These compulsions may have been indicative of Tourette's syndrome or obsessive-compulsive disorder. Ultimately, our family doctor diagnosed me with nervousness. He hoped that the symptoms would resolve themselves. For the most part, they did—but I remember how my brain and body felt during those anxiety-filled years.

I provide the above background to set the scene for a dark and depressing period in my life. Sometime around 2012, I started to suffer from extreme stomach aches. These weren't butterfly-in-your-stomach, uneasiness aches—they were completely immobilizing. They would onset unexpectedly, and we would be forced to cancel whatever activities we had scheduled. As they increased in frequency and severity, I was forced to see a doctor for help. After a consultation, I was diagnosed with anxiety and irritable bowel syndrome (IBS). I started taking medications that were prescribed for both diagnoses: citalopram for anxiety and omeprazole for IBS. While both changed the way I felt, neither caused the symptoms to subside. I tried to explain that there was something else going on, but the doctors dismissed my concerns. I wondered if my childhood anxieties were somehow to blame—if I were making it all up in my head.

I started to pay attention to my diet, mentally noting what I ate and how I felt afterwards, in hopes that I could control the sudden rush to use the restroom. But my symptoms progressed, and I was still unable to determine what exacerbated them. Soon, I started to become anxious after eating, anxious that I would be hit with a sudden urge to empty my bowels and that the bathroom would be too remote for me to make it without accident. That fear, in turn, caused me to withdraw from all unnecessary social commitments, which deeply affected my relationship with Amanda. She was always a social butterfly; before my downturn, we were always being invited to gatherings with her family, friends, and co-workers. I often had a fun time with those people, too. But the occasions where I felt well enough to go were vastly outnumbered by the days I wanted to stay home.

For a while, I forced myself to go out even if I knew I was sick. Amanda deserved to escape the gruesome realities of her job, where dealing with death and child sexual assault were everyday norms. Those nights would almost always end in disappointment. We would arrive where we were going, settle in, mingle with the crowd, and typically eat a meal. Within a couple of hours, the familiar feeling would start. Deep and aching stomach contractions would lead to a visit to the restroom. I started to notice that when my stomach hurt that bad, I would break out in a sweat. My throat would start to feel constricted, and breathing normally would become harder. This was followed by blurry vision and uncontrollable shaking. The smell of the room would turn acrid, and the sounds would become muffled. Only after relieving myself would the symptoms start to subside.

Those episodes usually led to me to force Amanda to leave prematurely. Ruining her fun was never my intent, but my health issues started to form a rift between us. I could feel the strain on our marriage. At some point, my incessant complaining led her to become dismissive of what was going on. Each time I told her how I felt, she would tell me to either go to the doctor or stop complaining. Each time I returned to the doctor, they, too, dismissed what I was experiencing. "It sounds like you are having panic attacks. Just relax and keep taking your medicine." "Just relax," as if

I hadn't spent my entire life battling anxiety. It was the best medical care I could afford to get.

Over the next few years, my affliction took a turn for the worse. One evening, Amanda was at work and I was at home with a very young Gracie and kindergarten-aged Joey. Stomach issues caused me to rush into the bathroom. Soon, I felt an overwhelming sense of impending doom, and I started to lose my vision. I ran out of the house and climbed into the passenger seat of the car, where I passed out. Unaware of what had happened, Dad pulled up to our house to see the doorway open, a frantic Joey on the front lawn, and me, completely oblivious to the world, lying face down in the car. Dad described to me my state when he arrived: "You were foaming at the mouth and shaking. I couldn't get you to respond to anything. I just pushed you all the way into the car and started driving to the hospital. I called the ambulance and told them to meet me on the way. I drove as fast as I could to get you to them. I thought you were dead!"

My heart broke that evening. Apparently, Joey was out in the yard unsuccessfully trying to rouse my unconscious body. I wish I could erase that memory from his mind. It must have had a lasting effect.

Once at the hospital, I started to feel a little better, but my stomach would hurt until I was able to defecate. MRI, EKG, and EEG tests were run on my brain and heart. Before testing was complete, I started feeling somewhat normal. I was released from the hospital without an answer. My official diagnosis was vasovagal syncope and anxiety, and treatment was follow-up with a primary care physician.

It took a few days for me to recover from the episode. I prayed that it would be an isolated occurrence. I had no idea what was wrong, but I knew that it was not just anxiety or IBS.

I avoided most food during the next few months as I continued to be checked out. My primary doctor wrote my hesitation off as anxiety-induced and told me to try to de-stress. In my line of work, de-stressing is practically impossible. Our lives were also undergoing significant, stressful changes that year: we were moving to a new home, and I was opening my own law office. The financial uncertainty brought about by these endeavors only worsened my illness.

Not long after moving into our new house, it happened again. Late one evening, after I had eaten a meal of lasagna, I awoke to find myself in a familiar predicament. I rolled over in bed and told Amanda that something was wrong. She responded by asking, "What's the problem this time?" By her tone, I could tell that she was frustrated that I had interrupted her slumber.

"My stomach is killing me," I replied. Our bedroom was located in the basement at that time, and I ran toward the stairs to climb up toward the ground-floor bathroom. After the first four steps, I lost all awareness. I thumped off the wall and onto the floor, and the sound must have alerted Amanda. "Mike! Are you okay?" she screamed. Unconscious, I was unable to answer.

I have tried to make sense of what I perceived that evening. I vividly remember the out-of-body, spiritual experience that I had while my body lay unresponsive. As the light of the world around me was being extinguished, I felt not fear, but a deep peace. While my eyes were closed to external stimuli, the normal darkness did not set in for long. From that blankness, a light approached me. It was the brightest white I had ever seen. It approached me not from one direction, but engulfed me from all directions, simultaneously. It brought with it warmth and a soul-quieting calm, a welcome distraction from the pain my body was experiencing.

Separated from the chaos that was taking place inside my body, I was compelled to remain in this state.

For a while, I floated there, somewhere between ignorance and understanding. I can't say that the events of my life began to flash before my eyes—they didn't. But there was a flash; somehow, a jolt of energy permitted me to think one unadulterated and complete thought about an absolute purpose for my life. I thought of my children, and them being without their father; and with that thought, it was implied that I had a choice. I could continue existing in this peaceful separation, or I could return to my failing and suffering body. I considered the former. In retrospect, I may have sacrificed my chance at heaven, as I understood that was where I was headed. I hope that was not the deal that I struck, but I still would have made the choice to return to my family. As I was pushed back toward my terrestrial existence, I knew that this tranquil respite was at an end.

As I woke up, I felt Amanda's arms shaking my limp body. Fearfully, she demanded, "Mike—wake up." The stomach pain had alleviated some, but my face hurt, my body was shaking uncontrollably, and my nose flared violently in reaction to a pungent odor that filled the air. A 911 call had brought medical responders to our home, the first of many made in response to my condition. As I was being strapped to a backboard, I listened as Amanda described what happened. "He woke up with a stomachache. As he went upstairs to go to the bathroom, he collapsed. I ran over to him, and he was foaming at the mouth and shaking. I noticed while it was happening that he went to the bathroom on himself. I tried to clean him up as best as I could." I was helpless. Gracie and Joey had been woken up by the noise of the ambulance, and I watched my little kids cry as I was wheeled away. If the previous event broke my heart, this one destroyed the fragments. Every ounce of dignity remaining in my soul was lost.

As we traveled to the hospital, I started to feel better. They were able to ask me some questions, and I was subjected to a similar routine as last time. The pain in my mouth was caused by the fall. My lips were busted open, and my front tooth was broken in half. I was given the same tests, which yielded the same results. I thought about how embarrassing the event might have been had we been in public, and those thoughts caused me to withdraw further from society.

I prayed that God would fix me. I still had work to do on earth. After being told repeatedly that my ailment existed only in my mind and was perpetuated by my own thoughts, I started to question my sanity. Maybe my mind *was* causing this.

Because we had just bought a house and could not make ends meet on Amanda's salary alone, I had to continue to work as best as I could. Typically, if I didn't eat anything, I would be all right during daytime hours; after eating, I was completely useless. Because of the cost of a hospital visit, Amanda attempted to handle the next few attacks that I had at home. Convinced that it was in my head, she tried to talk me through the episodes. Hearing her voice did help, but that help wasn't enough to prevent my body's standard response. "It's just anxiety, Mike," she'd say, her voice laced with a mixture of concern and exasperation. "Just breathe through it." I knew she was trying to help, but her words felt like a dismissal of the very real physical torment I was experiencing.

I was unreliable at the office. It took my body a couple of days to recover after an attack, days in which I would have to cancel appointments and court appearances. To make sure I could keep the lights on, I had to start accepting appointments as a Guardian Ad Litem. A GAL is appointed by the court to represent children in cases where abuse or neglect is alleged. They are responsible for investigating the matter and making recommendations to the court regarding the best interest of the children involved. That role changed the trajectory of my life.

The court appointed me to be GAL in a contentious child custody case. There were specific allegations of medical neglect lodged toward the dad by the mom, and allegations of mental disability lodged toward the mom by the dad. I spoke with the dad first. He indicated that the mom was a conspiracy theorist who believed that their child was allergic to meat, and that she accused him of risking the boy's health by forcing him to eat meals containing red meat. A burly, salt-of-the-earth type, this cattleman described his ex-spouse as delusional and disregarded her theories.

By the time I met with the mother, her ex-husband had convinced me that she was suffering from psychosis. Nevertheless, she came to our meeting seemingly put-together and lucidly described her child's situation to me. "He was bitten by a special kind of tick called the Lonestar tick. It has a dot on its back," she began. Because of my experience hunting and fishing, I knew exactly the type of tick she was describing. "That bite caused him to become allergic to red meat." I studied her face to gauge her level of commitment to this implausible connection—her expression showed complete sincerity. It was too unbelievable for me to digest, however. My mind was made up: she was suffering from delusions.

Committed to disproving the condition, I gathered more information from her. I asked for the name of the doctor that had made such a bizarre diagnosis, fully expecting her to tell me that she had done her own research and made it herself. Unexpectedly, she fired away: "Dr. Boatright. His office is in Farmington. He is an allergist. He has done multiple tests and diagnosed my child with Alpha-gal syndrome, which is an allergy to the carbohydrates in mammalian meat. Would you like his number?"

I quizzed her about the signs and symptoms of this allergy. She continued the lecture: "Two to six hours after eating red meat, the symptoms begin. They can range from a mildly upset stomach to anaphylactic shock and death. Usually, in our situation, it starts with a rash and leads to diarrhea. My child has started reacting to fumes from the cooking of meat, too."

Something clicked in my head. An upset stomach? Shock? Diarrhea? These symptoms sounded all too familiar. By the end of the meeting, I had gone from concerned to intrigued. After she left my office, I could not call Dr. Boatright quickly enough. Graciously, he accepted my call and answered every question I had. He confirmed the diagnosis and reiterated exactly what the woman had just told me.

Armed with that information, I was able to convince the dad that this was a legitimate health condition. Now, the parents share custody, and the father takes all necessary precautions to accommodate his child's illness.

On that first call with Dr. Boatright, I revealed my personal connection to the case, and we decided an office visit for some testing would be a good idea. At the visit, I got some more information. Dr. Boatright asked, "Have you ever been bitten by a tick?" "Doc," I responded, "I live in the woods. I hunt and fish and spend lots of time outdoors. I probably have been bitten by a tick at least one time today." He chuckled as we continued to discuss the limited amount of research regarding the tick bite exchange that causes this affliction. Dr. Boatright conducted a blood test and sent it to the only laboratory that tested for the malady, a private lab in Virginia. We spoke about the rarity, and how less than ten thousand people in the world have been confirmed to have the disease. At his insistence, I did not eat any mammalian products as we awaited the blood test results. Those results came back positive. I was diagnosed with Alpha-gal syndrome, or AGS.

Shockingly, turning away from mammalian meat products has eliminated the medical issues that I had suffered from for years. That random appointment, and Dr. Boatright's diagnosis, quite literally saved my life. For over ten years now, I have not intentionally eaten any red meat. I am what they call "dairy tolerant," meaning that I can handle limited amounts of dairy.

Many times, I find myself in the shoes of that young mother in my office—being interrogated, and having to defend my diagnosis to the skeptics. The burdens associated with AGS are not just turning away strips of bacon or a juicy steak. Cooking fumes from prohibited products can cause reactions. The aroma of barbequing meat induces swelling in my throat. I must constantly carry epinephrine. Eating out is hard, and trying new things or eating at new places cause tremendous anxiety. Family and friends have gotten used to me asking about the ingredients in their secret recipes. My own family has committed to eating mostly chicken, turkey, and fish to accommodate my restrictions. Many times, I have had to abstain from eating at work-related events, because it is easier to say that I am not hungry than to explain my bizarre affliction and risk sounding delusional. Even now, a decade after the diagnosis, I sometimes catch a flicker of doubt in people's eyes when I explain my condition.

The sacrifices that those around me have been forced to make because of my diagnosis are not lost on me. They are forced to cook with separate utensils and pans. They have to read labels meticulously. They warn me when something containing red meat is brought into our house. I am underserving of all they have done to respect my circumstances.

My sickness almost cost me my marriage. I understand Amanda's frustration with my never-ending stomachache. I understand her being dismissive and thinking everything was in my head. I understand her not wanting to be a full-time caregiver to a spouse in her thirties. But I just wish she would have listened when I told her that something else was wrong. For better or worse, she has inherently trusted every other decision that I have made for our family. She has let me take chances and trusted the process even when the goal seemed unlikely. The Alpha-gal diagnosis changed everything, not just my diet; it was validation, an assurance that I was not crazy. It allowed Amanda to become my advocate, rather than my skeptic.

Reassured that my mind and body were working properly and that my suffering was not self-inflicted, I was able to mentally, physically, and spiritually return to normalcy. I refuse to believe that random chance brought about the diagnosis.

THE WEIGHT OF MERCY

A couple years before my Alpha-Gal diagnosis, my mom and dad reconciled. It started with them casually talking at one of my kids' birthday parties. Despite never legally divorcing, they had lived separately from each other for a few years. Dad had remained with his girlfriend for a while, attempting to take part in Dustin's life. Mom had never tried to find another mate. While she had been hurt by Nicky, she still longed for the protection he had once provided her. Kevin and I shunned Dad, but somehow, Mom still wanted him.

After a sufficient number of those causal birthday meetings, Mom and Dad rekindled their relationship. Just like before, when Dad was with Gina, Mom was the other woman; when Dad began to focus on her, his primary relationship dissolved. With Dustin and his mom moving out of the house, Barb moved back in. I wanted both of them to be happy, but I doubted whether that was possible in a relationship with each other. Both remained addicted—Barb to Nicky, Nicky to prescription opiates.

I had stopped calling Dad a long time ago, tired of the broken promises and the constant disappointment, but I knew his health was getting bad. He had been using pain pills for years. Mixing them with Adderall provided the escape from the mundane that I believe he was searching for. Obviously,

Kevin and I weren't enough incentive for him to be sober. I still regret that we were apparently never enough for him.

As Grandpa Nick could no longer take care of himself, he and Grandma Janelle made a decision that would forever separate our family. He announced to us on one random afternoon that he was selling his house and giving the proceeds to Dawn so she could buy a new one about forty-five minutes away from Dad. Grandpa was going to move into the new house with Dawn, where she would take care of him.

That news sent us all into a frenzy, especially my dad. Dad had never lived more than a few minutes away from Grandpa Nick—for most of his life, he lived just next door. The older Nick provided just enough oversight to keep the younger Nick from stumbling over the edge of the cliff, but he also enabled the drug-seeking and drug-using behaviors of his son.

The philosophy was that if a doctor prescribed the medicine, it couldn't be that bad. If you had a headache, here was a fix—it was that simple. Dad had been hurt many times and had been legitimately prescribed pain medications. Grandpa Nick had injured his back when he was younger and also kept a supply of opioids on his person, all of which were prescribed. Grandpa played the game, rotating from doctor to doctor, and had amassed a hefty harvest of "feel good" pills. Grandpa's friends and family only had to ask and he would slide them a norco or an oxy. Kevin and I, though, never partook. We promised each other that we would never use any drugs—we had seen firsthand how devastating they can be.

As Grandpa moved away from Dad, Dad moved farther away from sobriety. The downward spiral was so bad that he had essentially cut himself off from the world. Dad felt like

Grandpa had abandoned him, so Dad abandoned everything and everyone. I remained in contact with my mom, but I ceased communicating with Dad during that time.

He lay on his side, body trembling as his muscles stiffened and released. His body shook violently, and then fell still. His breathing was shallow, and I dreaded that each exhalation would be his last. He had been like that for hours, but, selfishly, I wanted him to hang on. He was my closest companion, my hunting buddy, my protector, my catch partner. I wrapped my arms around his lifeless body and, believing it could be the last chance I would get to tell him, whispered, "I love you!" I wanted him to know that I valued his role in my life, and that, until his final moment, I was there.

The paragraph above describes two different instances in my life a decade apart. The latter of them was when our family golden retriever, Ranger, neared the end of his life. The former was when my dad tried to wean himself off of prescription opioids and Adderall. As I held Ranger in my arms, I couldn't help but think of my dad, and the many times I had watched him suffer through his battles with addiction. Both were trapped in bodies that were failing them, and I was faced with the agonizing decision of how to ease their pain.

I had begun writing this memoir when Ranger started to experience convulsions and seizures. The first time it happened was two days before he died. I was working late and came home to Amanda and the kids inexplicably babying Ranger. He was an affectionate animal, but he didn't desire the type of attention that most lap dogs seek. Acknowledgment and the occasional bone or piece of bacon would fill his cup. I inquired with the family regarding his new status, and Amanda explained, "We almost lost him today. He started having seizures. I laid him on his side and held his head. He shook for a long time. I almost took him to be put down. After I got him to drink some water, he started doing better. Eventually, he perked up and started wagging his tail."

"Wow!" I thought as I looked down at the seemingly unfazed canine. I noticed then that his face was no longer the golden color of his body, but was now almost entirely white, only a few isolated hairs poking through to hint at his previous color. I couldn't help but contribute to the royal treatment he was receiving. Ranger had been a great friend. We got him when Gracie was young, and he was her unsworn protector since the two first met. His allegiance wasn't just to the baby of the family: if anyone was out and about on the farm, he followed next to them like their shadow. He was my confidant, and many times, on the banks of our pond, as I fished and he used the water as his personal cooling station, I told him about my successes and failures. Whenever I landed a fish, he would rush toward me with the same excitement I had experienced catching it.

I knew his hourglass was running light on sand. We vowed to call the vet the next day to see if he could figure out what was plaguing our elderly pet. Ranger seemed fine that evening, and when we retired to bed for the evening, he was up playing with our other dogs. The next day would be the last of his life.

Amanda woke up before me that morning, as was customary in our home. She yelled up from the basement, and the concern in her voice caused me to quickly rise out of bed and rush to her side. For a brief time, we hoped he would recover from the seizures as he did the day before. When they lasted for over an hour, I called the veterinarian and begged for help.

As I described the symptoms and his state, the vet impressed upon me the harsh truth. "I'm sorry, but your dog is dying. He is suffering. He needs to be put down. If you bring him to me, I will take care of him." Based upon my body language while I listened to the diagnosis, Amanda could sense what had to be done. I explained to her that we could take him to the office and let the vet handle it, but the thirty-minute drive there would mean another thirty minutes of suffering. As we both cried, I asked, "Do you want me to do it?"

I knew it was my obligation. I let her and the kids say their goodbyes. After she left the basement, I began to weep uncontrollably. I picked up his limp body and whispered to him that it was all right for him to let go, hoping that he would die naturally. As I rocked him back and forth on my lap, I started to hear him softly whine from the pain that his body was enduring. I resolved to end his suffering.

I wrapped him in a blanket and placed him into the back of our side-by-side utility vehicle. I drove out to the most peaceful spot I could find on the farm, in the shadow of a cedar tree, and placed his body onto the ground. I grabbed the pistol from the front of the side-by-side and took aim. As I trained on his head, I hoped for a miracle. I even called his name a few times, hoping he would snap out of it. But he didn't.

Just before I pulled the trigger, I consciously adjusted my aim and fired a shot high, hoping that the explosion of gunfire would snap Ranger out of his fit. That didn't work either. His body remained nearly lifeless, soft sounds of pain the only trace that he still held on. I would not miss with the next shot. Immediately after I pulled the trigger, the noise stopped. There was stillness, soon followed by his tail raising up and wagging a couple of times: a friendly wave goodbye and a final thank you for ending his suffering. It had to be done, but I hated that moment. It was the hardest thing I have ever done.

The other incident occurred about a decade ago. Out of the blue one day, Mom called me frantic and distraught. She needed me to get to their house immediately. Dad was not breathing well, and he was barely responding. As I raced to their house, I knew he had overdosed. I began to think about how I could explain to my kids that their grandfather had died. I certainly would not be able to tell them the truth.

I entered my parents' house, and then their bedroom. Dad lay in the bed, disheveled and sweating profusely. The air in the room was thick with the smell of addiction and unwashed sheets. Mom explained, "I've been trying to get him up for a couple of hours. He just shakes and moans. His breaths are really shallow. He isn't responding to my voice."

"He is trying to quit his pain pills," she continued. "He said he was done yesterday, and he hasn't taken one since." I had evaluated the situation incorrectly. He had done the opposite of overdose. However, his abstinence was becoming his undoing. After researching online, Mom and I established a makeshift detoxification clinic. Sometime during the next two days, the scenario played out between my dad and me.

He lay on his side, body trembling as his muscles stiffened and released. His body shook violently, and then fell still. His breathing was shallow, and I dreaded that each exhalation would be his last. He had been like that for hours, but, selfishly, I wanted him to hang on. He was my closest companion, my hunting buddy, my protector, my catch partner. I wrapped my arms around his lifeless body and, believing it could be the last chance I would get to tell him, whispered, "I love you!" I wanted him to know that I valued his role in my life, and that, until his final moment, I was there.

After about seventy-two hours, Dad's condition started to improve. Eventually, he returned to normal health. He had quit pain pills cold turkey.

I was proud of his accomplishment, but it turned out to be short-lived. As is the case with most addicts, his addiction has followed him through life. Even with the use of suboxone, he cannot fully kick the desire to live life through opioid-tinted glasses. But he's still here, and some days are better than others. That's enough for now.

MANAGING A CAMPAIGN

Over a decade into my career as a prosecutor, one of the judges that I had worked with my whole career announced his retirement, and no heir was apparent. After some deep discussion, thought, and prayers for guidance, I decided to run for Circuit Judge of Division 2 of the 42nd Judicial Circuit of the state of Missouri. My near-death experience a few years prior had clarified the priorities in my life. Primarily, I valued my role as a protector, and as a judge I would be privileged to continue providing a voice for the voiceless and making my community safer.

Before I ran, I was the prosecuting attorney of the smallest county in our circuit. The 42nd Judicial Circuit is made up of Crawford, Dent, Iron, Reynolds, and Wayne counties. Because of the sparse population centers within the jurisdiction, I was viewed as the underdog from the day I announced my candidacy, especially against opponents like Brandi Baird, a former judge, and Steve Paulus, a well-funded attorney from the biggest county in the circuit. Undeterred by that classification, I traveled to Jefferson City on the last Tuesday in February of 2020 and officially filed to run in the election.

The first hurdle I had to clear was ballot placement. It is believed that placement first on the ballot can provide a five-to ten-percent vote boost, because undecided voters typically just go with the first option. First standing on the ballot is a very coveted position. Every person who had filed to run for office would draw a random number from a bucket, and the candidate with the lowest number would be placed first on the ballot.

The Jefferson City elections office was abuzz the day of the drawing. In the lobby where the line formed to file for office and participate in the number pull, statewide election officials mingled with candidates and the media. Even though a part of me tried to convince myself I had no business being there, I didn't feel like an outsider in that room. I casually chatted with Governor Parson about his law enforcement background and how my wife was also a police officer. I talked to Lieutenant Governor Kehoe about our shared involvement in the used car business. With Attorney General Schmidt, I discussed the realities of life as a rural prosecuting attorney, and how his office could help prosecutors like me. Unexpectedly, those men gave me the time of day, and their acceptance of me in that setting was all the validation I ever needed. I was where I was supposed to be.

The final event of the day was the number pull. As was explained to me, there were twenty-five hundred random numbers in the bucket. I would need to reach in and pull one out. I watched as a candidate for state representative pulled his number in front of me and showed the election official. "Number 138. That's a good one," she replied to the grinning man. Anxiously, I reached my hand into the bucket and shuffled the numbers around. I pulled out a small piece of folded paper. I unfolded the sheet and saw two zeroes and a one.

As I handed the worker my slip, I tried my best to bottle the childlike giddiness I felt. The worker announced to me, "You won the lottery!" The proclamation was heard by everyone in the large room, and a moderate contingency began to applaud—affirmation, again, that I was in the exactly right place at the exactly right time. I couldn't help but think of Dad and Grandpa Nick's lucky number seventeen that won them Table the Motion all those years ago.

I was going to be first on the ballot, but I had no idea how to run an election of this size. There were approximately fifty-thousand voters in the district, spread across five counties. The time it takes to drive from the southeastern-most portion of the circuit to the northwestern-most portion is three and a half hours. I was going to have to get organized, with haste. I was going to need someone for help and motivation; a guiding presence, but not a "yes-man." There was no better person for the job than my brother. Kevin had always told me the truth, even if it hurt my feelings. I knew I could count on him for this role—and I very much did.

Until we were in high school, Kevin was my "little brother." Since then, I have cautioned against using that language. By his freshman year, he began to dwarf me. In height, he was at least four inches my superior. During that campaign, he was gigantic.

To make an omelet, you've got to break some eggs. The COVID-19 lockdowns of 2020 broke many, many eggs over the course of my campaign. During the lockdown, businesses were not allowed to open. The courts were also closed for some time, and used exclusively for remote hearings for some time after they reopened. Those restrictions left me with a great deal of time, time I mostly spent on improving the hobby farm we were building. Specifically, we converted an outbuilding into a barn and built stalls to house our riding horses when they weren't in the pasture. Caring for our stock was a welcome escape from the mental prison the lockdowns had put us in. We were able to be outside, have purpose, and ride horses to distract us from the all the uncertainty in the world at that time. But while I was mucking stalls, Brandi and Steve were finding new ways to connect with voters virtually.

Playing farmer was nice, but it was doing nothing to further my campaign. In my mind, reaching out to voters through social media was all I could do. I made a daily Facebook post and answered any questions people had. Deep down, I knew that would not be enough for me to win the election, but it was something. That something was not enough for Kevin.

One morning, I was using a green John Deere tractor we had purchased with stimulus money to bring a large bale of hay to the pasture for the horses to eat when Kevin pulled into our driveway. He jumped out of his vehicle with a scowl on his face. I killed the diesel engine of the tractor so that I could talk to my brother. As soon as the engine noise quieted, he barked at me. "What are you doing?" he demanded. "Do you think you're fucking Farmer John?" I responded, with disrespect to match his, "What do you expect me to do?"

Before he left, he made his displeasure with my campaign strategy known. "You haven't done anything!" he shouted. "You are going to lose this election!" That was a tough to hear—but necessary. A yes-man would have agreed that I was doing all that I could and accepted that fate. Kevin refused. Not even a pandemic was excuse enough for him. He wanted me to win. His frustration with my campaign motivated me to action. I completed the feeding and called Kevin soon after.

I admitted that he was right: if I were going to win, I would have to outwork the other four candidates. I had to get out earlier, stay out later, and accomplish more than my competitors. That "Farmer John" comment helped me refocus my energy. It also confirmed that Kevin was in my corner. He was not going to let me lose, and I was not going to let him down. From that day until the vote was counted, we devoted every waking minute to accomplishing our goal. In total, we attended over one hundred events and knocked on over ten thousand doors. We went to town halls (wearing masks and standing six feet apart, of course), county fairs, and even the local rodeo, where I awkwardly tried to connect with voters while wearing a cowboy hat two sizes too big. Our tactic was divide and conquer: Kevin took one group, I took another. We focused on the issues that mattered most to rural voters: protecting our farms, supporting law enforcement, and upholding conservative values. We even created a catchy campaign slogan: "Randazzo: Protect your family, protect your property, protect your future."

Many people supported me privately, but their private conversations did not provide my campaign with a public presence. Other than the occasional helper (whom I very much appreciated), the main campaigners were Kevin, Treasure, Mom, Dad, Amanda, and Kevin's and my kids. Even though his health had deteriorated, Grandpa Nick provided what assistance he could. Because he couldn't walk without a walker, he rode around with my dad and helped identify good sign locations. As he had previously, time and time again, he gave every bit of himself to help me. I remember the day I gave out my first campaign shirt: it was to Grandpa Nick. I watched as his blue eyes went misty and swelled with pride. Seeing his name with the words "for Circuit Judge" next to it was something he could never have fathomed. It went without saying, but he took pride in the path I had chosen.

We worked hard that summer. As a result of the collective effort, I won the election with a plurality of thirty-six percent of the vote. My closest competitor got twenty-nine percent. As the results came in, I was greeted by all of my people. I embraced Kevin, and we both began to cry. We had accomplished something remarkable. I made a promise that evening to never forget how I had gotten there, and vowed to always express appreciation for anyone who has helped me along the way. Most judicial candidates win with a majority of the vote, a point that Judge Benjamin Thompson pointed out at my swearing-in ceremony: "You won an election where two thirds of the voters wanted someone else to be their judge." Although his words seemed harsh, Judge Thompson wanted to ensure that I didn't get too big of a head, something a friend of his kind is welcome to do.

With the victory, I became Circuit Judge Michael Randazzo on January 1, 2021. As I raised my right hand and swore to uphold the Constitution, I couldn't help but think of all the people who had helped me get there. As I embraced Grandpa, I knew we both must have been thinking about history. He had lived long enough to see the all the different phases of our family's evolution, but this was something new. The Randazzos had gone from juvenile delinquents to a judicial debutant.

THE WEIGHT OF A PROMISE

By the time of my election win, Grandpa Nick and Grandma Janelle were no longer physically or financially able to take care of themselves. They lived a transient life, floating back and forth from Dawn's house to Mom and Dad's. As Grandpa began to lose mobility, his once-steady gait became a shuffle, and he relied increasingly on a walker to navigate even short distances. He also lost mental acuity. The sharp mind that had once made countless deals at the Carlot began to fade, acuity replaced by confusion and forgetfulness. No one was willing to take the business over in his stead, and without Grandpa Nick's genius, the Carlot was no longer a money-making venture. Grandpa was forced to abandon the love of his life. Truthfully, his decline began in earnest when the Carlot went out of business. That decline was a slow and painful one; heart attacks, loss of consciousness, and a couple of head injuries from falls brought him near death.

In December 2021, the original five of us that shared that pop-up camper got to live together for the final year of Grandpa's life. Amanda and I had purchased another farm down the road from our house, where we planned to build a home. Kevin and Treasure would also be building their dream home at this new location. It was less than two miles down the road from our existing house, and we didn't want to sell the farm that our hard work had built.

The plan was for Mom and Dad to move into our old house. Because we were in the middle of a pandemic and the prices of building materials were significantly inflated, we were forced to wait to build—but we had already promised my parents that they could move in. And so, with us still in residence, Mom, Dad, Grandma Janelle, and Grandpa Nick moved into our house. Jacob had moved out at that point, but Amanda, Joey, Gracie, and I watched our household double in size.

While it was not ideal, the situation worked out better than expected. Grandpa required around-the-clock care, and having the whole group in the home assured that someone would always be there with Grandpa. Dad quit his job to be home and care for Grandpa, while Mom worked to pay their bills. Grandma and Grandpa survived off social security. Amanda and I agreed to pay all the household expenses while we stayed there.

I am so grateful for that year I got to spend living with Grandpa Nick, but it was a year full of suffering. I watched as Dad battled his addiction. Some days, he was vibrant and willing to face the realities of Grandpa's condition. Others, he would not get out of bed. I never quite figured out how he was continuing to get the opioids that he was abusing, but there was no shortage of doctors willing to write prescriptions for him. Grandma was healthy enough for a woman of eighty years, but she was unable to do much for Grandpa.

Mom had her own battles. She was severely depressed. In the last few years, she had lost her own mother and sister to cancer. I watch her battle that depression still today. When she wasn't working, she would help with Grandpa, too. Amanda, the kids, and I would also help when needed. Knowing that his time was growing short, I would have done anything to provide him with a little comfort.

Grandpa's good days were worth all the bad ones. I soaked in every single moment that I could. I asked him to tell me stories, details about his life. Some of his stories I heard for the first time; others, I already knew by heart. Even in those cases, I never asked him to tell a different one. I asked a lot of questions about our past, because I knew that we would be losing an unrecoverable wealth of knowledge when he passed away.

As Grandpa's health failed, we discussed his desire not to be relinquished to a nursing home. It was understood that, once he was placed in hospice, he would die at home. I made him a solemn promise that I would not let him die in a nursing home. I broke that promise, and it is the greatest regret of my life.

At this point, each of us was essentially working non-stop to keep up with his care, and hospice recommended we send him to a respite care facility for a break and reset in the home. Honestly, it was needed—everyone was exhausted. While we all agreed that it would be productive to get a chance to refocus, I was tasked with discussing it with Grandpa and getting him to agree to go to the nursing home for a few days. He agreed under one condition: I had to promise that he was coming back home. He would be at the facility for a couple of days. I'd go see him each day, and he'd be back home in three.

The first day I went to see him, he didn't seem to be in too bad of a shape. He asked me for a Dr. Pepper and some macaroni and cheese. I tracked his requests down at the local grocery store and returned to the facility, soda and pasta in hand. Mom and I fed him slowly and in small bites so that he was able to swallow without choking. Completely bedridden at that point, he needed our help to bring the soda to his lips and to drink it. We talked for a bit that day, and I reassured him he was one day away from coming home. He said he felt tired, and I watched him nod off to sleep. I hugged him tightly, and as I left the room, I said, "Grandpa, I love you!" I waited for a response, and, not hearing one forthcoming, I yelled, "Grandpa! I! Love! You!" He shook his head and slightly opened his eyes, and then he said what I believe are the final words he ever spoke: "I love you too, baby!"

I left the facility thinking about all the preparation we had to do for his return home. We were planning to make whatever his new favorite meal was, as his preference changed based upon the day. I went about the remainder of my day checking off tasks to make him as comfortable as I could upon his return to the house.

The next day, Mom and I arrived at the facility excited to bring him back home. I was hoping he was in a period of lucidity and we could talk about life, laugh together, and get his meal order for the evening. I remained in the parking lot to take a phone call. Mom went ahead into the facility. No more than thirty seconds later, I watched her exit the front doors, weeping. I dropped the phone and heard her utter the words, "He's gone!" Hoping she was mistaken, I ran into the facility and into his room. Grandpa Nick lay motionless on the bed, mouth wide open, with no sign of life. His body was cold to the touch. As some workers entered the room, I wondered, "Why aren't they tending to him? How long has he been like that? When was the last time they checked on him?" Behind all the immediate questions, I thought: "I broke my promise!"

Nick Randazzo's death passed onto me the burden of leading our family. I resolved to lead us in a new direction, but promised also to honor the family principles that he never let me forget. I thought about his unwavering loyalty, his fierce protectiveness of those he loved, and his belief in the importance of hard work. In the years since his death, I've tried to embody those qualities in my own life, both as a judge and as a father. I've also made a point of sharing his stories with my children, so that they can know and appreciate the legacy of their great-grandfather. He may be gone, but his spirit lives on in the values he instilled in us. As flawed as he was, his heart was always in the right place, even if he cared more about potential benefit than about legality. Despite his flaws, he made me everything that I am.

THE EULOGY

Grandpa Nick had always treated me as his own child. He treated my kids the same way. As he aged and his health declined, he often engaged in playful banter with them. In the 1990s, "yo' momma" jokes became entrenched in popular culture. The jokes always began with, "Yo' momma is so…" after which followed some derogatory description, such as, "so hairy that Bigfoot takes pictures of her." From time to time, Grandpa Nick would tell the kids his favorite yo' momma jokes. However, later in life, he used the phrase as a way of introducing himself, or announcing one of his grandchildrens' exits. Gracie played that game with him often. When she walked in the door, the race was on to say the magic words. Many times, he won. "Yo' momma! Yeah, yo' momma," Grandpa Nick would say before Gracie could beat him.

The days after Grandpa died were a blur. I knew that I was going to be tasked with speaking at the funeral. It was expected of me, and frankly, I didn't trust anyone to honor him like I would. It was a tremendous burden to summarize his life. In doing so, I had to reflect deeply upon my past. I hated the world for the way it had treated my Grandpa Nick; he had been quickly discarded after he had outlived his usefulness. The goal of this speech was to disregard any of the negative attributes he might have had and focus upon his positive characteristics. It is weird how we tend to do that when people pass away.

The service was held at a small funeral home where Grandpa Nick had purchased a pre-arranged funeral many years ago. The pews were packed with family, friends, and acquaintances, all gathered to pay their respects to a man who had touched so many lives. The air was thick in the cramped space, and abuzz with hushed conversation. As I stood at the podium, looking out at the sea of faces, I felt a lump in my throat, and a wave of emotion washed over me.

"I know my grandpa deserved for me to get up here and blow you away with my words. I don't have the mental acuity or the physical strength to properly do that, so, bear with me.

"From an early age, we are told that our grandparents won't be around forever. Those of us fortunate enough to watch them grow older tell ourselves that, at some point, this life will exist without them. Knowing that day will come, we strive to absorb every ounce of their personality, wisdom, and history.

"I truly have been at a loss for words. I've been recorded as speaking over one hundred thousand words in a day at court, but the hardest thing I've ever had to do was find the right words to honor my grandpa. I came to the realization that our language does not contain the proper descriptors, so I'll do my best.

"His personality was infectious. He had a way of lighting up even the darkest rooms, even in the hardest times. He was always quick with a joke or a kind word, and he had a genuine interest in the lives of others. And while he never received any formal education, he was the smartest person I know. He had street smarts and a common sense that you just can't learn in a classroom.

"Family remained his priority from his birth until his death. I find it impossible that any of you here don't know that. I believe Olive Garden owes him royalties because he fashioned the phrase, 'if you're here, you're family.'

"Some of you know the story, but I'll make sure you hear it again. As an infant, I lived with my mom and Dad, and Grandma and Grandpa in a camping trailer. My first Christmas was approaching, and there was no money to buy me a present. Grandpa decided to take action. He started driving over the road as a long-haul trucker. He left his last $5 with my parents and headed to California with a jug of water and some sunflower seeds, and left the order to 'get that kid something for Christmas.' From that point forward, he gave me everything I needed and built us a life that most couldn't dream of. Without him, there is no doubt I'd be standing in front of you all in an orange jumpsuit with 'Department of Corrections' on the back instead of a business suit.

"Almost every person here was helped by my grandpa. He was a magician that mastered the trick to making a dollar stretch beyond the limits of reality. I'm not sure anyone has ever helped more people with less money. Every dollar he ever earned was spent toward improving the lives of those around him. His door was always open. You never left his house hungry, sad, or broke. I remember one time when a family lost their home in a fire, Grandpa Nick organized a fundraiser at the Carlot, collecting donations and selling raffle tickets to help them get back on their feet. That's just the kind of person he was.

"Please never forget this amazing man!

"I promised I would honor his very last wish, so, to all of his grandkids…. yo momma!!!!"

During one of my last conversations with Grandpa Nick, I had promised him that I would speak at his funeral. I had also promised that I would tell Gracie "yo' momma" one last time. Not wanting to single out any of the grandkids, I said it to them all, but, without a doubt, Gracie knew it was meant for her.

After I finished speaking, there was a moment of silence, followed by a wave of applause. Many people came up to me afterward to share their own stories about Grandpa Nick and to thank me for honoring him in such a personal and heartfelt way. It was a cathartic experience, and celebrating the life of a man who had meant so much to me helped me to process my grief. I had been unable to fulfill my promise to not let him die in a nursing home, but at least I was able to honor his wishes and get Gracie one last time with a yo' momma.

THE ORANGE CROSS

During one of his days of clarity, Grandpa and I were alone in the living room talking. We spoke about life, regrets, and death. He explained that he was happy for the life he had lived. Despite not having any real material possessions left, he had everything that he wanted. He discussed his regret that he had never gotten to be a real mobster like his father, but that he wouldn't change that, because he knew that I would not have turned out how I did had his life been different. We talked about how much he cherished our relationship and how I was his hunting buddy.

I remember fondly my hunting trips with Grandpa. I recalled one particular time, when I was a teenager, we were deer hunting near the Iowa border. It was very cold out, and snow covered the ground. We ventured out to a prime spot and sat next to each other, each shivering but trying to wait out the other, each reluctant to be the first to admit that we really wanted to return to the car. The air was crisp and biting, and the silence of the woods was broken only by the occasional rustle of leaves and the distant call of a crow. Eventually, we did return to the car, which was parked on a trailhead not far from where we were hunting. Grandpa started it and turned the heat on. He reclined the front seat and instructed me to keep my eyes open in case a deer approached us. We both laughed and napped in the welcome heat of the car until it was time for us to return to camp.

In the living room, we talked about how he wanted to go back to Branson, Missouri one more time before he died. He didn't want to see a show or go shopping. No, he wanted to go to Branson for the food, and it was one place in particular: Whipper Snapper's. One year, we went to Branson for a few days. Grandpa, Kevin, and I were looking for somewhere to eat, and we found the perfect place. Whipper Snapper's was an all-you-can-eat lobster and crab leg buffet. It was extremely expensive, and we discussed the only way that we could go. The girls—Mom, Grandma, and Dawn—would not be able to eat enough to make it worth them going. Dad was not on the trip with us, as he was somewhere on his own adventure. It would be the three guys going to the restaurant. Grandpa knew we would have to eat a lot of lobster to make the price worthwhile. "Boys, don't go unless you're going to eat at least ten lobsters," he challenged. "It's a waste of money otherwise." Kevin and I were seafood connoisseurs, so the challenge was accepted. We went to the restaurant, took our seats, and began our gluttony. We filled the table and shoveled lobster after lobster into our mouths. I finished with twelve, Kevin with eleven, and Grandpa Nick with twenty-two lobsters. Grandpa Nick also ate three plates of crab legs. It was the most stuffed I've ever been in my life, and lobster still doesn't taste the same to me today. The sweet, briny taste of the lobster, the buttery richness of the crab legs, and the sound of Grandpa Nick's satisfied sighs filled the air as we devoured our feast.

We talked about death. I told him that after watching him suffer, I felt like I was losing faith in God. I asked him for a simple favor: "When you get to the other side, please send me a sign that God is real and that you are alright." After his death, I was hyperfocused on recognizing the sign, looking for some signal that he was reaching out. Little things would remind me of him, like a random Elvis Presley song or any time I saw a lobster. But nothing stood out as a definitive sign from Grandpa.

One evening last year, during deer season, I got my sign. I enjoy hunting now because it provides some mental relief from the hard decisions I make in the courtroom. The respite allows me to talk to God and to Grandpa. Each time I sit in the woods, I become the kid that sat in the warm car and enjoyed simply being in his presence. I almost feel like I'm sitting next to him. This particular evening, I only had about an hour to hunt. As I walked out to my stand with the hunting equipment that Grandpa gave me, I felt him near in a way that I cannot fully describe. It was as if a warm hand rested on my shoulder, and a familiar voice whispered in my ear. Other than the occasional dream in which he is brought vibrantly back to life, I haven't sensed his presence so physically. There in the woods, I did. I hadn't sat long when rustling in the brush alerted me to an animal that was looking on.

I stared down from my stand at an enormous white-tailed deer, antlers extending skyward. He was massive; in fact, he was the largest deer that I have ever seen while hunting in my life. Typically, when I see a buck in the woods, I struggle to contain my excitement. I have to focus on breathing, slow my heart rate, and steady my hands. This time, I experienced only calmness. I watched and waited for the right time, and then dropped the beast right where he stood. Excitedly, I approached the fallen deer and realized just how large the animal was. Unlike every other time I had harvested a deer, this deer grew larger and larger as I approached. I raced back to my house and enlisted Kevin to help me drag this monster out of the woods.

As we approached the buck together, the body again appeared to grow with each step. I gave Kevin my phone and posed for pictures, grabbing the deer by the antlers and raising his head toward the camera. Kevin took two photos, each from a different angle. After a struggle, we got the brute back to the house. Excited to brag about my accomplishment and show off the trophy, I opened the photos. As I looked at each, I could not believe what I saw. Each photo, although taken from different angles, contained a distinct orange cross on the horizon. Immediately, I knew this was the sign. It was too clear to be confused. It was Grandpa. There is a God, and my grandpa is all right.

That orange cross, emblazoned against the twilight sky, has become a symbol of hope and reassurance for me. It reminds me that even in the face of loss and grief, there is still beauty and meaning to be found in the world. It has strengthened my faith and deepened my appreciation for the bonds of family. And it has given me peace of mind, knowing that Grandpa Nick is still watching over me, sending his love and guidance from the other side.

FULL CIRCLE

When Joey graduated from high school, the administration decided to allow a guest to make a speech. It was the first time a guest commencement speaker would be included in the ceremony, and I was honored to be asked to give this address. This speech was to be my full circle moment. I have not included it in its entirety, as the omitted details are contained elsewhere in this memoir.

"Thank you all for allowing me to deliver this speech! For those who don't know me, I am Judge Michael Randazzo. I have known most of these young men and women since they began kindergarten. I have been known to them by various titles, but my favorite two have been: Coach, and Joey's dad. Almost exactly twenty-one years ago, I walked across the graduation stage here at this very school. Most people move away to find success; I found it at home. You can live anywhere on a map, but you can only be 'from' one place. Throughout my career, I have been proud to be from Bismarck.

"I want to tell you a little about myself; not to brag, but so you can all understand where I came from and where I ended up.

"My parents were high school dropouts. In fact, no one in my family had ever completed high school. I was born over a month premature, and I spent the first weeks of my life in the NICU. The doctors told my parents that I would be developmentally delayed, that I would be underweight, and that I would always require extra attention. The doctors didn't give me a chance. During the first year of my life I lived in a pop-up camping trailer, with no running water or electricity.

"In 2020, I was elected Circuit Judge of the 42nd Judicial Circuit for the state of Missouri. At that time, I was the youngest circuit judge in the state. In 2021, I was unanimously elected by the judges in my circuit as the Presiding Judge for the 42nd Judicial Circuit, making me the youngest serving presiding judge in Missouri; it is also believed that I was the youngest presiding judge in the history of Missouri's judiciary. I have also served over ten years as a prosecuting attorney, prosecuting and convicting over ten first-degree murderers. In all, I have participated in over seventy-five jury trials. I have appeared on various television shows and have made national headlines, most recently for my handling of the Josie Abney case in Salem, Missouri.

"You have now heard where I started and where I am now, but what is most important is how I got here. I grew up and was educated between these very walls. My picture hangs in the hall as the president of the class of 2003. Some of my teachers and classmates still teach at this school. My wife and children have attended this school for their entire educations. My son, Joey graduates here today.

"When I went to college, I received a full-ride academic scholarship to the University of Missouri-St. Louis, and I graduated from that college with honors. Bismarck is full of great teachers now, as it was then, and for me those years were easy. Struggles were on the horizon.

"I ask you all to indulge me in sharing a story you may have heard before. When Joey was in eighth grade, I was asked by the teacher of his Jobs for American Graduates class to talk to the class about my career.

"Before they entered the room, I placed envelopes containing a $2 bill under each of their chairs. When they came in, I told them to open them, look at what was inside, and tell me if it was legal tender in the United States. Almost every class member agreed that it was not real U.S. currency. At the end of the speech, I assured them that it was real and that it was theirs to keep, in hopes that they would retain the message attached to it. It was reported back to me that, coincidentally, an extra piece of pizza from the cafeteria was $2, and somehow the school ended up with about $60 in $2 bills.

"Now, the story. I started law school in the fall of 2007. A few weeks later, I had decided to quit. I had gotten a D on a paper, and a teacher had just told me the profession wasn't for me and that I ought to give up. Sitting on the floor outside her office, wondering how I was going to break the news to my parents that I was dropping out, a flyer for a speaking engagement caught my eye. A famed attorney who was part of O.J. Simpson's defense team was going to be giving a lecture that night."

(I had to pause the story here to provide some context to the kids. I gave a quick history lesson about O.J. Simpson, Robert Kardashian, and the "Trial of the Century." When I told them Kardashian is the father of Kim, Khloe, and Kourtney Kardashian, who are the sisters of Kendall and Kylie Jenner, it all seemed to finally click.)

"That evening, I arrived at the packed auditorium, expecting to hear wild stories about the Trial of the Century. I never heard a word about it. The lawyer spoke eloquently about his struggles with law school. He discussed how his road to law school was different than many of the trust-fund types who usually enter the profession. He described how he failed out of Harvard Law School but stayed resilient, and years later returned to Boston University Law School where he received the highest GPA in school history. He preached to us that we each have our own strengths and weaknesses, and that what the profession needs most are not cookie-cutter lawyers, but people with diverse backgrounds who want to work hard to accomplish their goals. He told us that we are all unique. He then asked us to reach under our chairs. I found an envelope, and inside was a $2 bill.

"The $2 bill is the oldest currency in still used in the United States. On the back it says, 'In God We Trust,' meaning that it is the oldest American document affirming our faith in God. It is a unique and sometimes unaccepted piece of currency, but it is every bit as valuable as all other currency, even if it is not as fancy as a $20, $50, or $100 bill.

"Kardashian's message resonated with me. I was motivated. I somehow salvaged my grade in that class and passed with a C. I was determined. God had intervened in my life. I continued my hard work and graduated law school in the top half of my class. I passed the bar exam on my first try. At my age, I have had an unparalleled legal career. All I have ever needed was a chance.

"I want my experiences to be a lesson to this class. Spend the extra effort doing ordinary things well, and you will transform into something extraordinary! When they are underwhelmed by your qualifications, overwhelm them with your work ethic! Work as hard as you can and be unique! Pray and let God guide you! Remember: when you are down to nothing, God is up to something!

"I read somewhere that speeches are supposed to have quotes, so I want to leave you with one from my favorite philosopher, Eric Church, from his song 'Talladega.'"

[The quote had to be removed due to clearance issues with lyrics, but the basic meaning of the lyrics were that there are few days in life that stand out. Those are the days that make life worthwhile.]

"Remember this day. It is one of life's most important milestones.

"It is such an honor and a humbling experience to share my story with you today. Thank you!

"To the graduates, your class holds a special legacy here are Bismarck. We are all rooting for you. You are all unique and valuable, even if we're not as fancy as some other places. I hope you retain that message. And finally—please take a look under your chair!"

Each chair had an envelope with a $2 bill inside taped to the bottom.

In the days and weeks that followed, I received countless messages from students, parents, and teachers who had been moved by my speech. Some said it had inspired them to pursue their dreams, while others said it had given them a new appreciation for the challenges I had overcome. It was a humbling experience, and it reinforced my belief in the power of storytelling to connect with others and make a difference in the world. I hope that Joey and all the graduates remember the message: anything is possible with hard work, determination, and a little bit of faith.

TATTOOS ON THE SOUL

Tomorrow, at the time I write this, I celebrate the completion of my fourth decade on Earth. I am not sure if I write because of my morality or my mortality, but either way these words are the unmitigated truth as I know it: a humble reflection on a life birthed into chaos, out of which has materialized law and order. A life spent attempting to remove labels.

Sewn into the fibers of my being is a proclivity to break the rules. I took a genetic test not long ago to ensure that I was in fact from these people, making sure each parent, grandparent, and ancestor matched. I have confirmation that they are mine and I am theirs. Regardless of what the results might have been, they are my family. They are my reason for being. In the breadth of my soul, I own all their misdeeds, traumas, and sins. I do not love everything that they have done, but I would make no substitutions in my life. My grandfathers were bootleggers and brawlers, my grandmothers were trapped in cycles of poverty and abuse. These are the shadows that have shaped my life.

Every man in my family that came before me was a felon, whether caught and punished or not. Every woman was a victim. I exist at the intersection of deviance and maltreatment. Despite the immorality contained within my DNA, I have endeavored to become a moral man.

To my progeny: I have attempted to remove every difficulty in my own life that could be replicated in yours. It has proved to be a vain pursuit. I can never fully wash you of the sins of this last name. Regardless, I would not be what I am if not for those sins. They are the burden that I carry, the tattoos on my soul. My sincere hope is that your generation is able to cleanse its conscience of the deeds of the past, and live the life that your own hard work earns you. I've tried to teach you empathy and compassion, and how to break the cycles of violence and abuse that have plagued our family.

I was never meant to be a writer. Hell, I was never meant to be much of anything. I am a consequence of poor choices, but I am not a victim of them. If anything, I am the beneficiary of dumb luck or undue divine intervention. This book is a critical look at the choices that allowed me to experience not just life, but a superb existence. If I die tomorrow, know that these forty years have brought me more happiness, success, and purpose than I could hope for in ten thousand.

To Jacob, Joey, and Gracie: you are my greatest works. To Mom and Dad: I am the best and worst parts of you both. Your love and nurturing gave me a chance. Somehow, God knew just how much chaos I needed in my life. Amanda, you put my life in order. You are the right amount of tough and tender. We have brought meaning to existence. Kevin, you are my best friend. We did this together. Grandma Sandy, I wish I had more answers about your beginnings. Grandma Janelle, thank you for teaching me to have faith. Your faith in God allows you to simplify the complex. You recognize the blessing in every situation and are never critical of others, even when they deserve it. Light to darkness. Order to chaos. All labels, removed. Grandpa Nick, I will never fill your shoes. I hope you get round two with that bear.

As I stand on the precipice of middle age, I am filled with gratitude for the life I have been given, and with hope for the future. May we all strive to break free from the chains of our past, and create a better world for ourselves and for the generations to come.

PHOTOS

*Picture of 2003 Bismarck High School Baseball Team
seconds after winning the district championship*

*Picture taken at Missouri State Softball Championship
in 2011. Left to right: Kevin Randazzo, Dominick
Randazzo Sr, Dominick Randazzo Jr, Michael
Randazzo (MVP), and Adam Randazzo*

*Picture of Uncle Michael Benigno courtesy
of St. Louis Post Dispatch*

Picture of Michael Randazzo on the bench

Picture taken of Michael Randazzo when harvesting large deer, with cross visible in picture. A sign from Grandpa Nick

Picture taken at my Swearing-In Ceremony for Circuit Judge on Jan 1, 2021. Left to right: Back row, Treasure, Kevin, Mom, Dad, Dustin, me, Joey, and Jacob. Front Row, Klarissa, Karson, Amanda, and Gracie.

Picture of my grandfather, Dominick Randazzo

Picture taken at Michael Randazzo's law school graduation. Left to right: Jacob, Michael Randazzo, Joey, and Amanda pregnant with Gracie

Picture taken of Randazzo Family left to right:
Jacob, Amanda, Michael, Joey, Gracie

Cruel and Unusual Punishment: A Memoir of the Psychological Realities of Federal Prison unveils the stark truth of an uncivilized, harsh, and insane system that erodes the very essence of humanity.